日本展望

ー教師用手引きー

Perspectives on Japan:
A Guide for Teachers

Rice growing in Japan is largely dependent on female labor.

Photo courtesy of Japan External Trade Organization (JETRO).

NATIONAL COUNCIL FOR THE SOCIAL STUDIES
BULLETIN NO. 69

Perspectives on Japan:
A Guide for Teachers

JOHN J. COGAN AND DONALD O. SCHNEIDER, EDITORS

Library of Congress Catalog Card Number 83-61859
ISBN 0-87986-045-6
Copyright © 1983 by the
NATIONAL COUNCIL FOR THE SOCIAL STUDIES
3501 Newark Street, NW, Washington, DC 20016

Contents

Foreword

This fascinating Bulletin will be a great help to all of us who feel an acute need to learn more about Japan so that we can better understand current events. *Perspectives on Japan: A Guide for Teachers* not only instructs, but also stimulates readers to want to learn more from other sources. In this Bulletin, one will discover unexpected similarities and unanticipated differences in our cultural perspectives.

This Bulletin offers excellent examples of some dimensions of a global perspective which are outlined in the NCSS position statement on global education: recognition that the human experience is globalized and that our lives are intertwined, that there are a variety of actors on the global stage, and that humankind is an integral part of the world environment. Clearly, the Japanese and American economies are intertwined. Multinational corporations, tourists, and visiting business-people are familiar global actors on both sides of the Pacific. Industrial pollution, non-renewable resources, and extinction of species are shared concerns.

Issues like these demonstrate another dimension of a global perspective—recognition of the links between present social, political, and ecological realities and alternative futures. Further, the NCSS position statement and this Bulletin together remind us that through our own and our students' actions as citizens, we can do much to promote better understanding between our peoples and to influence policies for the betterment of all.

As we teach about Japan and the Japanese people, students will realize that not everyone sees an issue from the same viewpoint. That recognition is a first step in the process of helping students to develop the capacity to view events from different cultural perspectives. International understanding is dependent upon the development of that perspective-taking ability. In order for peoples to be able to work together on shared global problems, they must be able to understand each other's orientation.

Teachers will find many opportunities in this publication for teaching powerful concepts and generalizations from history and the social sciences, for developing critical thinking skills, for practicing value analysis and decision-making, and for promoting effective social action. Thus, in teaching about Japan, we can work toward realizing the basic goal of social studies: "to prepare students to be humane, rational, participating citizens in a world that is becoming increasingly interdependent." At the same time, we can enrich our own lives through greater understanding.

On behalf of the National Council for the Social Studies, I want to thank the authors for giving us such an interesting and useful publication. Thank you, also, to those who worked on the Japan-U.S. Textbook Study Project, to the Japan Foundation, the Embassy of Japan, the Ministry of Foreign Affairs, The Ministry of Education, Science, and Culture, and the Keizai Koho Center (Japan Institute for Social and Economic Affairs), Japan Air Lines, and the office of Charles von Loewenfeldt. Together, you have done much to raise our consciousness and our desire to learn more about Japan. We are grateful to all of you for increasing our awareness and for helping us to better prepare our students for global citizenship.

We gratefully acknowledge the contribution by the Joyce Mertz-Gilmore Foundation and the Japan-United States Friendship Commission in partial support of this publication.

Thanks, too, to the continuing efforts of the International Activities Committee, the Publications Board, and the NCSS Publications staff. To all of you, "dōmo arigatō gozaimasu."

Carole L. Hahn
President

Preface

Let us stop the continents from hurling epigrams at each other, and be sadder if not wiser by the mutual gain of half a hemisphere. We have developed along different lines, but there is no reason why one should not supplement the other.

—Okakura, Kakuao, *The Book of Tea,* 1906

The plea of Okakura for the East and West to try to understand each other is as appropriate today as it was at the beginning of this century. All nations hold images of other peoples and places. More often than not, these images are biased, stereotyped, inaccurate, or simplistic. This is true of Japan and the United States. Although these two great nations are closely linked as political and economic allies, misunderstandings about each other abound.

Since 1977, NCSS has played an active role in trying to help teachers and other social studies educators to understand Japan. These efforts were undertaken initially through "study tours" sponsored by the Japan Foundation and JISEA, and, more recently, through the joint Japan-U.S. Textbook Study Project. In addition, the NCSS Annual Meeting in Portland in 1979 had a specific Japanese orientation, and the May 1981 issue of *Social Education* was devoted to the art and literature of Japan.

Still, some of us with a special interest in Japan believed that something more was needed—something tangible for the multitude of teachers who will never visit Japan. Accordingly, this Bulletin was conceived. It is intended to give classroom teachers several perspectives on Japan and the Japanese, as well as some ideas and resources for teaching about these perspectives. It makes no claim to be comprehensive; rather, it is a beginning. Our fervent hope is that these few pages will stimulate the reader to investigate topics and issues in more depth. Throughout the Bulletin, where appropriate, we have suggested further readings.

A number of individuals and organizations deserve recognition for their contributions to this publication. O. L. Davis, Jr., helped to formulate the original idea and undertook the first round of editing on a number of the substantive chapters. The NCSS Publications Board provided constant guidance for the project under the direction of three successive Chairpersons, Fay Metcalf, Janna Bremer, and Roy Erickson. The constructive criticism of the Board's "shepherd" for this project, Elmer Williams, was invaluable. The wisdom and practicality of Dan Roselle and Howard Langer helped to bring the Bulletin to completion.

Any project of this kind succeeds or fails according to the merits of its authors—not only their ability to write, but to follow outlines and make revisions within stringent deadlines. The authors of this Bulletin were exceptional in every respect. Special thanks go to Yoshiro Kurisaka, Yasuo Masai, Yoriko Meguro, Yasushi Mizoue, and Jiro Nagai, the authors of the initial substantive chapters. It is extremely difficult to write about complex ideas in a second language and to make the material concrete enough for teachers to use it in the classroom. These five scholars have succeeded admirably. Jackson Bailey deserves special mention for accepting the difficult challenge of commenting upon the chapters by the Japanese authors from an American perspective. Finally, Linda Wojtan's chapter on teaching ideas and resources should enable teachers to utilize the volume to its fullest extent.

In closing, we would like to dedicate this Bulletin to the children of Japan and the United States in the hope that its pages will give teachers the means to help them understand one another.

John J. Cogan
Donald O. Schneider

About the Authors

Jackson H. Bailey is Professor of History and Director of the East Asian Studies Program at Earlham College in Indiana. He is widely recognized for his historical and educational contributions to teaching about Japan. These include *Listening to Japan* (Praeger) and the video tape series *Japan: The Living Tradition* and *Japan: The Changing Tradition* (University of Mid-America). He spent the 1982–83 academic year lecturing and doing research in Japan.

John J. Cogan, co-editor of this Bulletin, is Professor of Education in the Department of Curriculum and Instruction at the University of Minnesota. He was a member of the 1978 NCSS/Japan Foundation Study Team. During the academic year, 1982–83, he was Fulbright Research Professor in International Education at Hiroshima University. He has written a number of articles on comparative and international education and social studies topics for elementary age children.

Yoshiro Kurisaka is Managing Director of International Affairs for the Keizai Koho Center (Japan Institute for Social and Economic Affairs), Tokyo. He has served as a staff reporter for the Asahi Shimbun, where he reported on economic and international affairs. He has also served as a correspondent in Washington, DC.

Yasuo Masai is Professor of Geography at the University of Tsukuba, Japan. Masai taught at Michigan State, Rissho University, and Ochanomizu University, and served with Japan's National Committee on Geography, the National Committee on Pacific Science, and the International Geographical Union.

Yoriko Meguro is Professor and Chairperson of the Department of Sociology, Sophia University, Tokyo. Meguro's special fields of interest are women's studies, social networks, and family relations, on which she has written extensively.

Yasushi Mizoue is Professor of Social Studies Education at Hiroshima University. He previously served as social studies specialist at the Ministry of Education, where he wrote the new social studies course of study. He has been a member of the Japan-U.S. Textbook Study Project. He has written widely on social studies topics.

Jiro Nagai is Professor of Education and former head of the Division of Social Studies Education, Department of Education, Hiroshima University. Long active in UNESCO's Association Schools Project in Education for International Understanding and other international education efforts, he is currently president of the Japan Social Studies Research Association.

Donald O. Schneider, co-editor of this Bulletin, is Associate Professor, Social Science Education Department, College of Education, University of Georgia, Athens. A member of the Board of Directors of NCSS, he has written extensively on global education and other social studies curriculum issues.

Linda S. Wojtan is Executive Director of The U.S.-Japan Education Group. She has served as the Assistant Director of the Japan-U.S. Textbook Study Project and is chairperson for the Committee on Teaching about Asia of the Association for Asian Studies. She has taught at high school and university levels, and has conducted in-service workshops. Publications include articles and curriculum materials designed to enhance the teaching of Japan.

This is the Yuji Furukawa family in Tokyo. They live in a three-bedroom apartment. He is a financial expert in an advertising agency.

Introduction

Japan in the Curriculum: Toward a Rationale for Teaching About Japan

DONALD O. SCHNEIDER AND JOHN J. COGAN

The steady growth of Japanese economic power in recent years has renewed American interest in Japan. The focus has shifted from the "curious" and quaint elements of Japanese culture to the institutions and elements of Japanese culture which might explain how Japan rose from the ashes of war to become a successful economic competitor. Whereas relations between the United States and Japan formerly attracted only sporadic media attention and held slight interest for most of the American public, they are now the subject of increasing concern to American government, business, and labor. This concern has manifested itself in subtly anti-Japanese television commercials, outspoken demands for trade restrictions, and public protests of Japan's economic "invasion."[1] There is danger that a kind of xenophobia may grow up, fostering an irrational perspective on Japan long after the immediate issues recede from public attention in the United States.

Invariably, such national attention will affect school curricula. Although an understanding of various issues involving relations between Japan and the United States is important for American citizens and youth, the issues themselves do not provide an adequate basis for systematic curriculum planning. A comprehensive rationale is needed—one that approaches current Japan-United States relations from a scholarly perspective, yet provides for instructional treatment appropriate to the capabilities of students and the larger interests of American society. Such a rationale must address several

---

[1]"Nissan Groundbreaking Disrupted," *The Atlanta Constitution*, February 4, 1981, p. 14A.

key questions. For what purpose will Japan be included in the curriculum? What will be taught about Japan? At what school levels? How will instruction be organized? What will it contribute to students' perspectives on themselves, the world, and their own society? We will address some of these questions briefly in this chapter; others will be treated in subsequent chapters. Let us turn first to what we know about the way in which children view their world.

The Perspective of Children and Youth on the World

Research indicates that children go through three stages in learning about the world.[2] In the first stage, which continues up to the age of seven (grade 2), children develop strong attachments to their own country, and a "we/they" perspective emerges. The second stage begins in the primary grades and continues into grades 4 and 5. In this stage, children's concepts about their nation rapidly become more sophisticated with the acquisition of abstract and ideological knowledge. By the age of nine or ten, positive feelings toward the nation, generated through acceptance of national ideals and internalization of symbols of national identity such as the flag and the Statute of Liberty, create a kind of "patriotic filter" through which children view their world. They screen out negative images of their nation and fear those perceived as political enemies who seek to change the status quo and disturb their homes and security.[3]

In the third stage of development, commencing in the upper elementary grades, children begin to view themselves and their nation as part of a larger organized system. Their typically positive attitudes toward their nation stabilize; perceptions and attitudes toward "foreign" nations, peoples, and ideas become fairly firmly established. Researchers have concluded that after about the age of 12, perceptions and attitudes become extraordinarily difficult to reorganize, and that middle childhood is therefore a "critical period" for developing an international or global perspective and accompanying attitudes.[4]

Although the International Association for Evaluation of Educational Achievement (IAEEA) Study of 30,000 pre-adolescents and adolescents in nine democratic nations indicated variations in the strength of national identity and other specific constructs, the pat-

---

[2] Richard Remy and others, *International Education in a Global Age, Bulletin 47* (Washington, DC: National Council for the Social Studies, 1975).

[3] Thomas Buergenthal and Judith V. Torney, *International Human Rights and International Education* (Washington, DC: U.S. National Commission for UNESCO, 1976).

[4] *Ibid.*

tern of development in children was found to be a common one. Variation in the nature and strength of views was found to be linked at least in part to schooling practices and to the society's other broader efforts at education of its citizens. For example, American 14-year-olds ranked near the top in their knowledge about domestic political institutions and processes, but near the bottom in their knowledge about international institutions and processes. Considering the lack of exposure to international content in most social studies programs and mass media in the United States, this is not surprising. (In a 1973 UNESCO study of television content, the U.S. ranked last among 100 nations in time devoted to international programs.)[5]

Similar deficiencies in knowledge about cross-cultural or global phenomena persist among college-age youth in the United States. Seniors averaged only 50% correct responses in a recent study measuring global understanding.[6] Patterns of misconceptions underscore the lack of attention in college curricula to topics such as environment, population, energy, human rights, health care, and food. These topics are not typically included in courses organized within traditional academic disciplines. In contrast, students performed better on questions dealing with content usually found in traditionally organized history, geography, and other courses.

It is apparent, then, that learning about other cultures and nations is related to children's developmental patterns; to those perspectives, ideas, and data valued most by different societies, and thus included in their educational systems; and to the nature and organization of various scholarly disciplines.

Different Perspectives for Teaching About Nations and Cultures

Several perspectives have been or continue to be advocated and employed for teaching about nations and cultures in elementary and secondary schools. Although variations and overlapping may sometimes blur distinctions among them, their identification may be useful in analyzing existing curriculum and instructional materials, and in selecting materials and planning instruction.

TRADITIONAL HISTORICAL PERSPECTIVE

This perspective includes those approaches and materials which focus on the development of individual political units or larger

---

[5]*Ibid.*

[6]Thomas Barrows and others, "What Students Know About Their World," *Change* 12 (May/June 1980): 10–17, 67.

"areas." Sometimes topics such as "industrialization" or "revolution" provide the organizing framework. A structure which combines chronology and topics is fairly common. Emphasis is usually on political, military, and international affairs, with some attention to geographic influence and economic developments. Recently, more attention has been given to social and cultural elements and to cross-national movements. By and large, non-Western cultures are viewed only in relation to the development of Western history, or as problems in United States foreign relations.[7]

TRADITIONAL GEOGRAPHICAL PERSPECTIVE

This perspective gives major attention to a nation's location, climate, natural resources, size and characteristics of its population, type and stability of its government, communication and transportation systems, and economic and technological development. It typically divides the world into regions and then national units. Formerly, descriptive/physical approaches prevailed; recently, more emphasis has been given to regional associations and human cultural factors.[8]

WORLD AFFAIRS OR FOREIGN POLICY PERSPECTIVE

A major focus in this approach is government-to-government relations; foreign policy, diplomacy, treaties, agreements, and other aspects of international relations are the major topics for consideration. The nation-state is viewed as the central force on the world scene and the center of individuals' political concerns. Therefore, it is the primary unit of analysis for understanding world affairs. Issues are selected and studied largely as problems in foreign policy. Cultural differences in institutions, customs, and traditions merit study largely as a means for improving inter-nation relations.[9]

CULTURAL PERSPECTIVE

Those critical of the more traditional disciplinary approaches to the study of other nations and peoples often argue for a broader

---

[7]See Part IV, New Perspectives in the Study and Teaching of World History, *New Perspectives in World History*, 34th Yearbook (Washington, DC: National Council for the Social Studies, 1964).

[8]James Preston, "The Significance of Geography in American Education," *The Journal of Geography* 68 (November, 1969): 473–483; Lorrin Kennamer, Jr., "Emerging Social Studies Curricula: Implications for Geography," in Phillip Bacon, ed., *Focus on Geography: Key Concepts and Teaching Strategies*, 40th Yearbook (Washington, DC: National Council for the Social Studies Sciences, 1970); Jan O. M. Broek and others, *The Study and Teaching of Geography*, Columbus, OH: Charles E. Merrill, 1980.

[9]James M. Becker, "The World and the School: A Case for World Centered Education," in James M. Becker, ed., *Schooling for a Global Age* (New York: McGraw-Hill, 1979).

and "other-centric" view of the world. They emphasize the importance of studying another culture from the "inside"—to look at a variety of cultural elements, including the arts, literature, folklore, daily life, and customs—and of using cross-cultural studies to understand our own society better. Advocates contend that to obtain accurate and non-stereotypic views of another culture one must apprehend it through the eyes and ears of its native members. This will bring about not only better understanding, they argue, but appreciation of human similarities and cultural uniquenesses.[10]

GLOBAL PERSPECTIVE

Educators concerned with "pan-human," international issues and with the increasingly global nature of our experiences argue that the cultural perspective—though more valuable than the traditional historical, geographical, or world affairs perspective—still provides inadequate preparation for today's citizens. According to these educators, national and human survival require the development of basic competencies, including the ability to perceive the world as a system, the capacity to make decisions and form judgments, and the capability of exerting influence. Content, they argue, should emphasize those concepts that represent enduring and significant phenomena such as *conflict, change, interdependence,* and *communication,* and issues that have global implications such as *war and peace, population limitation, distribution of food,* and *conservation of energy resources.* To avoid ethnocentric, "we/they" thinking, they contend, examples and illustrations of these themes should be drawn from several cultures.[11]

These are instructional perspectives on nations and cultures generally—not Japan specifically, or Asia as a region. Although the instructional treatment of Japan and Asia can be categorized using these general approaches, we can also identify some specific Asian perspectives.

[10]Verner C. Bickley and others, "Education for International Understanding," *International Educational and Cultural Exchange* 12 (Spring, 1977); Leon Clark, "The Middle East: From Headlines to Humanism, *Social Education* 42 (October, 1978); 444–447; Seymour Fersh, *Japan in the American Classroom* (New York: Consulate General of Japan, Japan Information Service, 1977); Seymour Fersh, *Asia: Teaching About/Learning From* (New York: Teachers College Press, 1978); Teaching Japan in the Schools, *East Meets West: Mutual Images* (Stanford, CA.: Stanford University, 1980), p. 1; Donald C. Wilson and Walter Werner, "Viewpoints in Global Education," *The Social Studies* 71 (November/December, 1980): 250–253.

[11]See for example, Robert G. Hanvey, *An Attainable Global Perspective* (New York: Center for Global Perspectives, 1976) and *Social Education* 41 (January, 1977), which includes a series of seven articles on this topic. See especially the articles by Gerald Marker, Charlotte and Lee Anderson and Donald Morris. See Lee F. Anderson, *Schooling and Citizenship in a Global Age: An Exploration of the Meaning and Significance of Global Education* (Bloomington: Social Studies Development Center, Indiana University, 1979); also Becker, *Schooling for a Global Age;* Raymond H. Muessig and M. Eugene Gilliom, eds., *Perspective of Global Education: A Sourcebook for Teachers* (Columbus: The Ohio State University, 1981).

APPROACHES TO TEACHING ABOUT ASIA

In the mid 1970s, the Asia Society conducted a study of approximately 300 social studies textbooks used in elementary and secondary schools in the United States. Reviewers found that these books take one or more of five basic approaches.[12]

1. *The Asia-Centered Approach.* This category included those textbooks which attempt to describe the reality of Asian societies from inside the culture, so that things and institutions are presented as normal, logical, and rational. Asians are not pictured as being "just like us," but are presented in such a way as to encourage a realistic view and student empathy. This approach was employed in 30% of the books, but was dominant in only 18%.

2. *The Progress-Centered Approach.* This perspective views change as necessary, inevitable, and essential for progress. Once an exclusively Western perspective, this view of the world has now come to be shared by Asians, claim proponents. Books in this category frequently provide treatment of economic conditions, technological change, and industrialization. This approach was reflected to some extent in 71% of the books.

3. *The Western-Centered Approach.* This perspective was found in 76% of the textbooks and predominated in over half of them (56%). From this ethnocentric point of view, authors portray Asia as "catching up" with the West, especially in political, economic, social, and scientific endeavors. The textbook authors tend to magnify the international roles of Americans and Europeans and to view Asia as a stage for the unfolding of Western history.

4. *Asia as Inscrutable or Exotic.* This formerly common approach focusing on the exotic, strange, and mystical ways of Asians was rarely found in the textbooks surveyed.

5. *Eclecticism.* While many textbooks unconsciously and uncritically adopted more than one perspective, only 5% were classified as truly eclectic.

Not surprisingly, the perceptions that might result from heavy reliance on textbooks pervaded by these perspectives can be found among students and the general public.[13] In a broader, more impressionistic assessment of teaching and writing about Asia, Donald

---

[12]The Asia Society, *Asia in American Textbooks* (New York: The Asia Society, 1976).
[13]James W. Boyd and Loren W. Crabtree, "American Images of Asia: Myth and Reality," *The Social Studies* 71 (July/August, 1980): 184–190.

Johnson has identified seven approaches, or, as he terms them, "levels of consciousness."[14]

1. *Asia as a setting for Western history.* Asian nations are barely perceived as national and cultural entities in themselves, but rather in relation to the unfolding of Western history.

2. *Asia as a problem in American foreign policy.* Asian nations are recognized as separate, distinct entities, but only because of their geopolitical impact on our lives and national policies.

3. *Anti-stereotype campaign.* Asian nations are recognized as entities valuable in their own right. Their development (modernization), is stressed and their idiosyncratic cultural elements are downplayed.

4. *"We are all human."* Peoples of the world are conceived as all very much alike, with the same needs and attributes. Empathy is created through understanding.

5. *Comparative social science process.* The study of all cultures is organized around selected analytic concepts and processes. Asian case studies form the focal study of universals (socialization, urbanization), rather than cultural uniquenesses.

6. *Cultural uniqueness orientation.* Individual cultures are examined within the context of their own aspirations, perceptions, and concerns, heightening consciousness of each Asian nation.

7. *"Asia, get to us."* Purely intellectual understanding subserves presentation of uniquely Asian outlooks, insights, and ways of thinking and behaving, because of their perceived value in teaching about universal human needs.

Johnson cautions that one orientation is not necessarily superior to the others and that distinguished scholars and teachers may be found who adhere to each. The majority of elementary and secondary educators, however, currently seem to espouse those approaches identified by Johnson as middle-level orientations. In particular, a global perspective seems to be in the ascendant in educational writing.[15]

---

[14]Donald Johnson, Service Center Paper on Asian Studies, No. 4 (Columbus: The Ohio State University, Asian Studies Project, 1972) quoted in Fersh, *Asia: Teaching About/Learning From*, pp. 24–26.

[15]James M. Becker and Lee Anderson, "Global Perspectives in the Social Studies," *Journal of Research and Development* 13 (Winter, 1980): 82–92.

Although advocates of a global perspective offer some powerful arguments for their position, it does pose some problems as a basis for organizing curriculum. One problem can be a diffuseness in attention to specific nations and cultures. In focusing upon topics or issues and drawing from a variety of cultures as illustrations, teachers may fail to provide students with systematic, in-depth study of nations and cultures. Students consequently may not develop a holistic view or "feeling" about another culture. Students need a balance between studying about topics or phenomena as they relate to several nations and cultures and the in-depth study of selected cultures.[16] Global education advocates acknowledge this point.[17]

Why Focus on Japan?

Systematic study of other cultures permits us not only to learn *about* other people, but also to learn *from* them.[18] This is exactly what the Japanese have done throughout much of their history—initially, through study of China, and more recently, through study of the West. Americans are now becoming more aware of the value of studying and adapting from others—in particular, Japan.[19] Japan has much to recommend it as one of those nations that might be most profitably singled out for in-depth study in the elementary and secondary curriculum. It exhibits many striking similarities to and fundamental differences from the United States.

As an economic superpower and the second most important trading partner to the U.S., Japan carries on economic activities which affect millions of Americans daily. In its material culture it has much in common with the U.S. and other industrialized nations. It also confronts many similar challenges, such as maintaining environmental quality, providing adequate housing and social services in its crowded cities, meeting energy needs, and controlling inflation. Although Japan has an old culture compared to that of the U.S., both became important actors on the world stage at about the same time. Other similarities are noteworthy. Since the U.S. occupation during World War II, Japan's parliamentary political system has been committed to fundamental democratic principles. The Japanese also share with Americans a work ethic, and most Japanese, like Amer-

---

[16]The Statewide Social Sciences Study Committee, *K–12 Social Science Education Framework* (Sacramento, CA, State Development of Education, 1968) proposed three modes of study: analytic, multi-setting study of a topic; integrative, single setting study of several topics; and decision making study of issues or problems.

[17]James M. Becker, "Needed: A Global Context for the Study of Nations and Peoples," *Georgia Social Science Journal* 12 (Summer, 1981), pp. 1–2.

[18]Seymour Fersh, *Asia: Teaching About/Learning From*, p. 2.

[19]See for example, Ezra Vogel's *Japan as Number One: Lessons for America* (New York: Harper and Row, 1980).

icans, achieve status through their work. Cultural exchange and borrowing have influenced both cultures. Typically, most Americans think about this cultural influence largely in terms of what the Japanese have borrowed and adopted from the West, and the United States in particular. But in architecture, art, poetry, and music, for example, the Japanese have influenced their American counterparts.

Although many similarities, mutual influences, and shared elements can be identified in the two cultures, superficial treatment may fail to help students identify the very substantial differences that exists in institutions, traditions, customs, and ideas. The world view of most Japanese is not, after all, the same as that held by most Americans. The Japanese think and feel differently about the world. The differences are well illustrated in our language patterns and ways of communication. Japanese indirectness in contrast to American directness, for example, is reflected not only in language, but in the way in which Japanese and Americans make decisions.

In summary, Japan is a good choice for in-depth study in the elementary and secondary social studies curriculum because it provides an opportunity for students to study a culture that can be both compared and contrasted to their own. Many things about modern Japanese society will seem quite familiar to them, but the cultural differences will also help students to view the same phenomena from a different perspective. Finally, Japan is a major actor on the world stage. Because it is a nation with which the United States is directly and increasingly involved politically, economically, and culturally, it is important that Americans become more knowledgeable about the nation, its culture, and its people.

What Should We Teach About Japan?

In planning this Bulletin, the editors considered contacting American authors who were specialists on Japan. However, it seemed preferable to ask Japanese scholars to write the substantive chapters dealing with Japan, because this procedure would provide American educators with a perspective from "inside" the Japanese culture that is not usually available to American elementary and secondary teachers. As the Japan-U.S. Textbook Study Project found, textbook writers in each society tend to emphasize different elements of each other's culture and history.[20] These differing perspectives are only natural. Awareness of those facts and perceptions about Japan that Japanese think should be presented to non-Japanese could provide

---

[20]The Japan-U.S. Textbook Study Project, *In Search of Mutual Understanding* (Bloomington, IN: Indiana University, 1981).

a useful comparison to what is typically found in U.S. textbooks and instructional materials. To provide such a perspective, five Japanese educators were asked to write brief chapters on geography, culture and history, economic development, the role of women, and citizenship education (Chapters One through Five). The reader should bear in mind that these writers are detailing what *they* believe is important about each of these areas—what *they* wish United States teachers to know about Japan.

This approach is not without its problems. An obvious one is that the authors are not writing in their native language. The structure of the language and the meanings communicated are very different. Finding English words that convey the exact meaning of a Japanese expression is sometimes difficult, if not impossible. Thus, the description of an event, era, or process known well among Japanese may, when translated, communicate far less to English readers than it does in Japanese to Japanese readers. Translation is not necessarily the central problem. The Japanese employ a wide range of shadings in meaning in their language. Some of these meanings can only be translated approximately into English. Such approximation is therefore a source of distortion.

A second problem with writing for a foreign audience is the possibility that the authors will consciously or unconsciously emphasize certain facts and gloss over or ignore others to present a favorable view of their own nation. In discussing Japan and its economic development, for example, Japanese often emphasize the relative smallness of their country, its lack of natural resources and the necessity to work hard and to trade sharply just to survive. On the other hand, Japanese are less inclined to discuss other factors that foreigners may see as equally important—a homogenous culture which outsiders find difficult to penetrate, government protection of some industries until they are highly competitive, and minimal expenditures for a military establishment that have permitted economic resources to be used for more productive ends. Emphasizing or ignoring such factors invariably results in interpretations that a non-Japanese may see as distortions.

A third problem is that Japanese writers may attribute many complex consequences to very simple facts. Thus, the fact that Japan is a "tiny" country with a large population may be elevated to a sort of grand explanation (or as some might contend, even an "excuse") for historical developments or current policies. Those Japanese who led Japan into World War II used the almost religious profession, "Ours is a small land," to justify territorial expansion. Although more subtly elaborated, the same fact is still used to justify Japanese economic policies of the last generation. The factual assertion must be viewed in two ways: (1) in a global context, where Japan's size is not as disadvantageous as the Japanese perception suggests, and (2) in a historical context, where the claim takes on added meaning in understanding Japanese perspective, motives, and policies.

These and other problems confront nonspecialist readers of the chapters authored by the Japanese writers. In some cases, the writers present factual information much as they might to a Japanese audience, leaving it to American readers to discern its meaning and significance. In other instances, such as in Nagai's discussion of moral/citizenship education in Japan, the information represents the Japanese setting, and a comparison to the United States context is not presented. For these reasons, we asked Jackson Bailey, a noted American specialist on Japan, to review the chapters by the Japanese authors and place them in context. His chapter—Chapter Six— should help nonspecialist educators to read the substantive chapters more critically and meaningfully.

The last two chapters focus on teaching activities and resources for elementary and secondary schools. Drawing on some of the key points raised in the substantive chapters, Schneider provides suggestions applicable both to elementary and secondary classrooms. In the final chapter, Linda Wojtan surveys some of the major resources available in addition to textbooks and lists organizations that distribute materials on Japan.

The purpose of this Bulletin is to provide an introduction and overview for those teachers who are not already familiar with Japan. It is a point of departure, rather than a comprehensive, sophisticated treatment. The editors hope that it will provide suggestions and perspectives that will motivate readers' further study of Japan and ways in which content about Japan may be appropriately and usefully included in the social studies curriculum.

Japanese respect for their ancestors is shown at the time of the fall equinox. It is believed that, in commemoration of Buddha's experience of Nirvana, hell opens and spirits of the dead are allowed to visit home. People gather in cemeteries to welcome the visiting spirits.

Photo courtesy of Japan External Trade Organization (JETRO).

日本人の日本展望

Part I
Japan from a Japanese Perspective

Ryozo Niikura is a fisherman who trawls the waters off Kanagawa prefecture. One of his problems is cleaning off the garbage that comes up in each haul, damaging his net.

Photo courtesy of Japan External Trade Organization (JETRO).

CHAPTER ONE

A Geographic Perspective on Japan

YASUO MASAI

Japan is an island country in East Asia. Its large population is concentrated in high density centers. Modern technologies and ways of life have found strong footholds in Japan's unique traditional culture, and the two ways—new and old—characterize contemporary Japan. East and West have been amalgamating.

Physical Setting and Area

Japan consists of four principal islands: Honshu, Hokkaido, Kyushu, and Shikoku. It also has hundreds of smaller islands. All of these are situated at the place where the world's largest continent—Eurasia—and the world's largest ocean—the Pacific—meet. This geographic setting has exerted a profound influence on Japan. In contrast to most of Asia, Japan is truly an insular country. Its national borders are all on the sea. That Japan has no land borders seems directly related to Japanese perceptions of international problems. Japan is sometimes depicted in Western books as if it were an England in Asia. Japan's insularity, however, should be stressed much more than this suggests. Although it contains some island stepping stones, the Korea Strait has a width of some 200 kilometers, about five times the distance of the channel separating England and France.

Most Japanese people consider Japan a small country. Japan has an area of only 377,420 square kilometers. A comparison of its land area with other countries of the world and states of the U.S. clarifies this conception of size (see Table 1). In fact, its size is much larger than the average for the 161 countries in the world.

One reason why Japan is very often perceived as a small country

Table 1.   Area Sizes of Countries and U.S. States, (In Thousands of Square Kilometers)

Countries	Land Area	States	Land Area
Japan	377	Alaska	1519
United Kingdom	244	Texas	692
West Germany	249	California	411
France	547	Montana	381
Italy	301	New Mexico	315
USA	9363	Illinois	146
Canada	9976	New York	128
China	9561	Pennsylvania	117
Australia	7687	Maine	86
Thailand	514	Massachusetts	21
Philippines	300	Hawaii	17
New Zealand	269	Rhode Island	3

Source: UN Demographic Yearbook (1979), U.S. Statistical Abstract (1980)

is that it is surrounded by huge physical regions such as the Asian Continent and the Pacific Ocean and vast national areas such as the USSR and China. The Japanese tend to think of the United States and Canada, two of the largest nations in the world, as their neighbors, since no other nations exist between Japan and them.

LANDFORM, CLIMATE, AND LIFE

Japan stretches 3,000 kilometers from the northern islands to Okinawa in straight distance, or 3,500 kilometers in curving real distance, in two major arcs of islands. Its topography is largely attributed to the Circum-Pacific Orogenic Zone, which stretches to the Pacific coast of the United States. This zone, known generally in the Americas as the Cordillera, normally is surrounded by sizable flatlands, plains, and basins. In Japan, however, flatlands are insignificant by American standards. Even the largest, the Kanto Plain, is nearly identical in area to the Delmarva Peninsula.

Japan is a mountainous country. At least 70 percent of its land is mountainous. Eighty percent can be labeled as mountains and hills where human beings cannot easily live. The remaining land area is either lowlands or slightly higher uplands and is largely cultivated or urbanized. The highest peak is the famous Mt. Fuji (Fujisan) (3,776 meters) and mountains higher than 2,000 meters are generally found in central Honshu. Even smaller mountains tend to have steep slopes, eroded by torrential rivers. Mountains in Japan look somewhat like the Great Smokies in the southeastern United States. Small mountain villages are perched on mountain sides, especially in southwestern Japan. Some high mountains have a little snow even in summer. Many of the famous mountains of Japan are volcanic, such as Mt. Fuji.

The climate of Japan ranges from subtropical to temperate. Its northeast to southwest chain may be compared with the stretch of land from Maine to Florida in climate as well as length. Precipitation is much greater in Japan than in the United States. Areas where annual precipitation is 1,000 millimeters, as in Georgia or North Carolina, are considered "dry" by Japanese standards. Most of Japan's heavily populated areas have about 1,500 millimeters of annual rainfall.

Japan's four seasons are clearly distinguished and winter brings frost and snow to most of the nation. Although not in high latitudes, about half of Japan gets snow which stays on the ground for weeks and months. Some cities and many villages in northern Japan are often covered with one to five meters of snow. About 20 mil-

Map shows Japan's size in relation to East Coast of the United States.

lion people live in the snow country facing the Sea of Japan and in Hokkaido.

The mountainous terrain and heavy precipitation make Japan's flora and fauna abundant. Wild bears, boars, and monkeys are found in the mountains only 50 or 60 kilometers west of downtown Tokyo. Mountaineering, hiking, skiing, and swimming are extremely popular recreational activities. Even the most inland city in Japan is only 100 kilometers from the nearest sea, and wherever one lives in Japan, except for the distant islands, mountains are visible.

Natural disasters are numerous in Japan. Typhoons sweep over this island chain several times every year, bringing with them floods and high winds. Typhoons have not caused extensive damage in recent years because of a nationwide system of levees. Instead the rain brought by typhoons is considered a natural gift which greens the country and cleans the rivers. Earthquakes are common in Japan, but are not often catastrophic. Once in a while, *tsunami* (tidal waves) hit indented coastal areas. Volcanoes erupt occasionally, but their damage is normally restricted to small areas. Land slides and avalanches are other types of natural disasters in mountainous areas.

People, Life and Culture

POPULATION

Japan now has about 120 million people, ranking seventh among the nations in the world after China, India, the USSR, the U.S., Indonesia, and Brazil. Japan's population increased rapidly from the Meiji Restoration of 1868 until recent years. During the 250 years of the Tokugawa Shogunate, which was characterized by feudalism and isolation from the rest of the world, Japan's population increased very slowly, hovering close to 30 million. During the last 100 years, the population of Japan has quadrupled. Some Japanese have emigrated to the Americas. Sizable Japanese enclaves have been established in Brazil and the United States, while naturalization of foreigners has been very limited in Japan.

Two prominent demographic characteristics of Japan are its population density and pattern of population distribution. Japan's population density is among the highest in the world. According to figures in the 1979 *UN Demographic Yearbook*, the population density of Japan (303 persons per square kilometer) is exceeded only by that of South Korea (364 per square kilometer), Bangladesh (559 per square kilometer), Belgium (324 per square kilometer), and the Netherlands (337 per square kilometer). The population is restricted largely to the island's small plains, narrow valleys, and basins. Since the total area of Japan's flatlands is comparable to that of California's Central Valley and Japan has such a large poplation for its size, the human habitat of Japan could be considered a large-scale experiment in preparation for the more crowded planet Earth of the future. With the population increasing throughout the world, Japan may have something to teach other nations about dealing with high population density and utilizing modern technology to make limited living space humane and appealing.

The ethnic character of the Japanese population is another unique feature of the country. Less than 1 percent of the 120 million people living in Japan are non-Japanese nationals. Koreans constitute most of these non-Japanese residents, although some Chinese, Americans, and Europeans are long-time residents. Practically all Japanese nationals are individuals whose family history cannot be traced back to foreign countries. In fact, Japan has only one minority ethnic group among the nationals—the Ainu, who now live in Hokkaido, numbering less than 20,000.

In the long course of its history, Japan received waves of immigrants from the continent and the Korean peninsula, from Southeast Asia and southern China by way of Okinawa, and from the West Pacific. Some may have come from eastern Siberia by way of Sakhalin. The geographical location of Japan to the east of the Asian continent in the northwestern Pacific washed by the warm Japan Current seems to have determined the destination of migrants in prehistoric and early historic periods. The Japanese Archipelago became a kind of terminus for these prehistoric migrations. The land received these various ethnic groups many centuries ago, and in time they became largely indistinguishable from one another.

RESOURCES AND INDUSTRY

Farming in Japan is characterized by small-scale operations. Arable flatlands are scanty, especially by American standards. The average Japanese farm is only slightly over one hectare, or about 3 acres, in size. Nearly 5 million farmers, of whom the overwhelming majority are part-time farmers, work these small farms. Yet, Japan's agricultural productivity per unit of area is among the highest in the world. This is to be explained by the (1) use of fertilizers, chemicals, and machines; (2) selection and improvement of crop seeds; (3) hard and diligent work of farmers; (4) relatively warm climate with high humidity; and (5) high prices of agricultural products as incentives to produce.

Recent production figures of major agricultural products are shown in Table 2. It is a well-known fact that rice is the most important

Table 2.   Major Agricultural Products of Japan (1979–80), (In Thousands
of Tons)

Rice	12,589	Wheat	367
Mandarin Orange	3,539	Barley	276
Potato	3,520	Persimmon	275
Sweet Potato	1,431	Soybean	111
Apple	959	Redbean	87
Japanese Pear	518	Rye	50

Source: Ministry of Agriculture, Forestry and Fishery, Japan, 1981.

crop in Japan today. Other cereals, such as wheat and barley, are also grown in Japan. Vegetables and fruits are cultivated in warmer climates and in metropolitan areas. Some fruits, including apples, are exported to other countries. The consumption of fruits by the Japanese population is quite high. Greenhouses abound in Japan, producing high-priced melons, strawberries, vegetables, and flowers. Major vegetables, in order of 1979 production volume, include diakon (big radish), cabbage, Chinese cabbage, onion, cucumber, tomato, eggplant, and others. Fresh vegetable salad is consumed in large quantity. Diakon and Chinese cabbage frequently are pickled.

Tea is grown fairly extensively in the southwestern half of Japan. Most of the tea harvested in Japan is processed into green tea. Large quantities of black tea are imported from India, Sri Lanka, and Taiwan. Other important special crops are rush, which is made into *tatami* cover, the woven mat floor covering still found in most Japanese homes, and *konnyaku*, a kind of root crop processed into a gelatin-like food.

Prior to World War II, most farmers were tenants, but now tenant-farming is rare. Some landowners, mainly those who own small tracts, ask other farmers to cultivate their land on contract.

Japan now imports many agricultural products, including many from the U.S. Wheat, corn, and fruits are imported in large quantities; much grain is fed to milk cows, beef cows, pigs, and chickens. Large-scale pastures in Japan are uncommon, except in Hokkaido.

Practically all the mountains of Japan are covered with trees. Varieties of evergreen broadleaf abound in southwestern Japan, deciduous trees grow in northeastern Japan, and coniferous trees are common in eastern Hokkaido and the high mountains of Honshu. Nearly half of the forests are the result of careful harvesting and replanting. Pines, cryptomeria (sugi or Japanese cedar), and other conifers have been planted extensively for several centuries. Japan is now regarded as one of the few countries in the world to be successful in reforestation. Lumber is still imported extensively, however, because most Japanese houses are constructed of wood. The United States, Malaysia, Indonesia, the USSR, Canada, the Philippines, and New Zealand are the major sources of lumber imports.

Fishing is very important in Japan. Although much of the catch comes from large-scale deep-sea fishing now extending even to the Atlantic Ocean, coastal fishing also flourishes. The picturesque coastline of Japan is dotted with small fishing villages. Local fishermen catch many kinds of fish—including shellfish, squid, octopus, and sea urchin—and gather seaweed for human consumption. Fresh seafood is very important since fresh raw fish is considered a delicacy. The rising living standards of the millions of Japanese have created an enormous demand for fresh fish. This demand is now satisfied only by supplementing local catches with frozen fish caught in distant seas. Local aquaculture of yellowtail, shrimp, oyster, and seaweed are other important marine activities in Japan. The cultivation of pearls must also be considered a part of the general harvest from the sea.

Fishing in Japan ranks first in the world both in quantity of fish and commercial value. Per capita consumption of fish by the Japanese is one of the highest in the world, but, interestingly, consumption of beef and other meat is increasing and now rivals that of fish.

MANUFACTURING INDUSTRY AND TECHNOLOGY

Large-scale Western technologies were introduced rapidly after the Meiji Restoration of 1868. Successive wars with China, Russia, and Germany (World War I) contributed much to the development of modern manufacturing industries. During World War II, Japan's heavy industry was completely destroyed. Postwar reconstruction produced a more varied and mixed industrial base. Today, Japan produces all kinds of manufactured goods—large and small, advanced and traditional. Japan's manufacturing industries now rank among the top in the world (see Table 3). In total value, they rank second only to the United States (manufacturing in the USSR ranks somewhat lower), giving Japan the second largest gross national product (GNP) in the world today.

Manufacturing industries are scattered all over Japan, but most industries are concentrated in a belt from Tokyo south to northern Kyushu and include the large cities of Nagoya and Osaka. This great manufacturing region can be compared to such areas as the New York State/Great Lakes region in the United States and the region along the Rhine in Western Europe. Today, most towns and villages in Japan have some kind of manufacturing industry. In many cases,

Table 3.   Japan's Ranking in the World's Manufactured Goods (1979)

Automobiles	1	Television Sets	2
Cameras	1	Zinc	2
Shipbuilding	1	Aluminum	3
Cement	2	Electricity	3
Chemical Fiber	2	Glass	3
Computers	2	Pulp	3
Paper	2	Soda	3
Plastics	2	Steel	3
Synthetic Rubber	2	Sulfuric Acid	3

they are subcontracting factories which produce parts for the larger plants. Some factories in South Korea, Taiwan, and Hong Kong also produce parts or assemble manufactured goods under contract with Japanese industries.

Industries often pose major environmental problems. Stringent regulation has reduced air and water pollution, but these are problems which still remain "unsolved." Construction of large factories destroys natural and cultural beauty. Especially problematic is the seacoast, which can be transformed by oil storage tanks, chemical plants, steel plants, docks, and warehouses. Since large factories are difficult to construct in densely populated areas, coastal sites are preferred. Here, raw materials can be imported and manufactured goods exported more easily. Large factories and large cities are commonly located along the Japanese seacoast.

MINING AND ENERGY

Japan has traces of many mineral resources. However, economically exploitable natural resources are scarce. Virtually every natural resource consumed in Japanese factories and homes must be imported. Of the major items consumed, the degree of foreign dependence is as follows: iron ore—99 percent, copper ore—86 percent, lead ore—64 percent, zinc ore—59 percent, bauxite—100 percent, tin ore—96 percent, nickel—100 percent, coal—77 percent, petroleum—99.8 percent, and natural gas—73.9 percent.

The energy issue is a critical one in Japan. Most of the energy consumed is supplied by oil, almost all of which is imported. The growing oil consumption by both factories and homes must be reduced through a variety of means, including conservation efforts. Coal reserves are not scarce, but mining Japanese coal is extremely difficult and its quality is low. This necessitates major importing of coal from Australia, the USA, Canada, the USSR, South Africa, and Vietnam, among other nations.

Hydroelectric power is another important source of energy, but it presently represents only 5.1 percent of the total energy supply. In 1960, it was 15.3 percent. Construction of large dams is expensive in Japan, where mountain gorges are very steep. Yet, abundant small dam sites in Japan have promise, since the electricity generated can be conveyed to markets over short distances.

Today, about 15 percent of Japan's electricity is generated by nuclear power plants. These plants are located at coastal sites. They have met strong opposition at times, but more are under construction. The nuclear raw materials are imported—primarily from the United States and Canada.

Volcanoes provide geothermal power on a small scale. Some wind and wave forces are being utilized for generating electricity, but this capacity is not yet large. Solar heat is omnipresent in Japan. Water warming devices have been installed on roofs of millions of houses. The relatively large windows of Japanese houses make possible the intake of solar energy into rooms in winter. Compared to the United States, however, Japan's per capita consumption of energy is not large because of its more concentrated population, smaller houses, and more common use of public transportation.

URBAN AND RURAL LIFE

Japan is a rapidly changing nation, as is the daily life of the Japanese. It is almost impossible to generalize about daily life in either urban or rural areas. Contrasts of urban and rural, modern and traditional, and large and small characterize Japanese culture today, resulting in multiple dimensions of daily life.

Nevertheless, 90 percent of the Japanese work in cities, and most of them live in cities. Ten cities in Japan have a population of one million or more: Tokyo (8.5 million in the city; 11.6 in the Metropolitan Prefecture), Yokohama (2.8), Osaka (2.6), Nagoya (2.1), Kyoto (1.5), Kobe (1.4), Sapporo (1.4), Kita-Kyushu (1.1), Fukuoka (1.1), and Kawasaki (1.0).

The greatest urban concentration is the Tokyo Metropolitan Region with a population of more than 25 million within the 50-kilometer radius from downtown Tokyo. This is one of the largest urban population concentrations in the entire world. The urban life of the Japanese is well represented by the people of Tokyo Metropolitan Region, which constitutes over 20 percent of the total population of Japan.

Most of the city people of Japan are commuters. Tokyo's downtown is much like that of other great modern cities in the world. High-rise buildings dot most of the downtown. Commuting is normally accomplished by trains, including subways and elevated railroads, but a considerable number of commuters use private cars and buses, together with bicycles and motor bikes. Trains are often very crowded during rush hours. In very exceptional cases, people called "pushers" are employed to push commuters into jammed trains. In such circumstances, most commuters cannot find a seat and must stand to their destination. Many commuters need more than an hour and a half for commuting each way. In the Tokyo Region, the average railroad commuting time is about one hour in length. The Japanese railroad network is very well developed and the trains are modern and clean. The term "shuttle service" may be applied to Japanese commuter trains in large urban centers. Trains run frequently; in some cases, a train of about ten cars arrives and departs every two minutes. In metropolitan residential areas, commuters and shoppers park hundreds—even thousands—of bicycles near a station, causing severe traffic problems. Yet, the bicycles are not disturbed throughout the day.

In contrast to the congestion of Tokyo, smaller cities, towns, and villages in the countryside are automobile-oriented, even though rail and bus routes serve them. At the same time, the government is rapidly extending the length of one of the world's fastest train services, the *Shinkansen*, or New Trunk Line, in order to connect many local cities of Japan with the large metropolises. As of June 1982, the *Shinkansen* served 12 of the 13 largest cities of Japan directly. About two-thirds of the total population of Japan lives in a belt stretching from Tokyo on Honshu to Fukuoka on Kyushu, an area about 1,000 kilometers long and 50 to 100 kilometers wide. From the inauguration of the *Shinkansen* in 1964 to 1980, the train had carried more than a billion passengers. It helps to create a great megalopolis with a population of more than 50 million between Tokyo and Osaka-Kobe. Were Fukuoka and other cities and towns included in the urbanized belt westward from Osaka-Kobe, some 80 million people would live in this area.

Japan is a mobile society. People commute, travel, and change their residence often. Place-rooted social patterns have been altered considerably. This is most noticeable in the large cities. Yet, even from remote mountain villages and isolated islands, migration to the large urban areas is substantial. Occasionally, the populations of entire villages have moved to urban areas, although roads now link such mountain villages, and the villagers have their own cars and motor bikes. Urbanizing villages are confronted with social conflicts between new and old inhabitants whose values are often very different.

Since land in Japan is limited, and the average size of farms around great cities is 0.5 hectares, or only slightly larger than one acre, the acquisition of large tracts of land is generally impossible. The price of land is extremely high. The urban house, in turn, cannot be large. The average floor space is about one-third that of the average American urban home.

A typical Japanese urban house may have three or four rooms, plus a kitchen, a bathroom, and a toilet. It is usually constructed of wood and has a tiled roof. A suburban house is usually surrounded by a small yard planted with bushes, trees, and flowers. In congested areas, the yard is often occupied by garage space for a car or bicycles. Courtyard-type houses are practically nonexistent in Japan—a large difference from Chinese or Korean urban houses. While Japanese yards may be very small, they are frequently decorated by artistically trimmed trees and carefully arranged rocks.

Traditionally, the Japanese sit on the floor to eat, talk, and meet people, and they also sleep on the floor, using quilts and mats. A traditional room floor is made of *tatami*, a type of bamboo mat. Sleeping quilts and mats are stored in closets during the daytime, so that the space may be used as a guest room, a play room, or a study room. Recently, the use of Western-style furniture such as chairs, desks, tables, and to a lesser degree, beds, has become common. Wooden flooring has become more common than in the past and carpeting is sometimes used. Nearly all homes have a TV set, washer, and refrigerator. Stereo sets, pianos, electric ovens, cars, and many other modern items abound. Even computers of a small size have found their way into Japanese daily life. The number of TV sets and automobiles per capita is actually higher in rural areas than in cities. It is a well-known fact that Japan produced more automobiles than did the U.S. in 1982. This helps to explain why the automobile is no longer a luxury in Japan and why many families have two cars. Japan is an increasingly affluent society.

Urbanization often leads to problems and criticism. The Japanese people complain about the smallness of the houses, the narrowness of the roads, the congestion of the trains, and the relatively high prices for many items. "Laissez-faire" urban planning, crowded recreational areas and facilities, and the noise caused by traffic and factories are other problems which are frequently discussed. In addition, the fear of earthquakes or typhoons is always present.

Japan is a nation of Buddhist and Shinto faiths. Most Japanese belong to both religions and ceremonial life is traditionally related to both religions. Most houses have a Buddhist and a Shinto altar. Clearly many Japanese are devout Buddhists and Shintoists. At the same time, secularism prevails among the Japanese people. Temple and shrine visits are often regarded as recreational or educational activities rather than religious events. Only one percent of the Japanese are Christians.

Education plays a major part in Japanese daily life. Compulsory education continues for nine years. Most children normally take part in education outside the school. Especially in cities, most children go to authorized or unauthorized private cottage schools, institutes, or homes to receive additional tutoring in preparation for the major exams. Small ones, called *juku*, meet two or three times a week. Even on Sundays or national holidays, these schools or *juku* absorb hundreds of thousands of children. In rural areas, the trend is not as conspicuous as in cities. For students who wish to enter universities, preparatory schools provide special opportunities for increased learning.

These private schools (many large preparatory schools are authorized by the local governments) teach all subjects which are taught in public schools. In addition, calligraphy, painting, music, gymnastics, sports, dance, flower arrangement (*ikebana*), tea ceremony (*chanoyu*), and yoga are taught.

Sports attract millions of Jananese. Baseball may be the most popular professional and amateur sport. Volleyball, basketball, soccer, tennis, golf, Ping-Pong, bowling, and many others are also played. American football and handball are becoming popular. *Sumo*, or Japanese wrestling, attracts millions of Japanese television viewers. Judo is very common, too. Many citizens also participate in *kendo* (Japanese fencing), and karate. Other very popular sports or recreational activities include mountaineering, hiking, skiing, and swimming. Here again, Western influence is very strong; yet, many traditional sports are enjoyed, too.

Cultural activities are varied. Visits to museums, zoos, botanical gardens, and art galleries are popular. Large cities have a variety of such cultural institutions, but smaller cities generally do not. Many libraries exist, but their capacity is limited. Urbanization has destroyed many traditional houses; old villages and townscapes have been renovated. Cultural lectures or cultural schooling (adult education) aimed primarily at housewives and salaried men are becoming popular all over Japan. Compared to the United States, the role of the universities and schools in adult education is quite limited. In the countryside especially, the elementary and junior high schools play important roles in the social and cultural life of villages. Sports days (physical education) or class days (e.g., music, drama) attract large numbers of local citizens.

Japan once had many language dialects. During the course of modern history, political and educational efforts have been made to standardize the language. In many cases, standardization has been achieved through schooling and mass media. Now, practically all Japanese can comprehend standard Japanese satisfactorily, even though many people still have clearly recognizable dialects.

Summary

Japan's geographic location has contributed historically to its self-imposed isolation. But during the past century this isolation has virtually disappeared, as noted by Reischauer:

> Japan, in fact, is in a sense the least remote of all nations today. None is clearly more dependent on a massive worldwide flow of trade simply to exist. As a result, it has developed strong trade relations with almost all parts of the world. The seas that once cut it off now bind it effectively to all regions. The great distances that once lay between it and all other countries have now shrunk to insignificance. . . . The shift from almost complete isolation little more than a century ago to complete involvement today has, in historical terms, been sudden. . . .[1]

The Japanese are faced with a new role in the continually emerging world order—one of leadership. With their geographic location no longer a paramount factor in relating to other nations and people, their human and economic resources now allow the Japanese to assume a leadership role in Asia and throughout the world.

---

[1] Edwin O. Reischauer, *The Japanese* (Cambridge, MA: Belknap Press, 1978), p. 37.

REFERENCES

Association of Japanese Geographers, ed., *Geography of Japan*. Tokyo: Teikoku Shoin, 1980.

Association of Japanese Geographers, ed., *Japanese Cities—A Geographical Approach*. Tokyo: Association of Japanese Geographers, 1970.

———. *Japanese Geography 1966—Its Recent Trends*. Tokyo: Association of Japanese Geographers, 1966.

Bureau of Statistics, *Statistical Yearbook of Japan 1982*. Tokyo: Government Printing Office, 1982.

K. Yano Memorial Society, ed., *Nihon Kokusei Zue* [A charted survey of Japan]. Tokyo: The Society, 1982.

Masai, Yasuo, *A Comparative Study of Japanese and American Cities*. Tokyo: Kokon Shoin, 1977. (In Japanese with English abstract)

CHAPTER TWO

Japan's Cultural Tradition in Historical Retrospect

YASUSHI MIZOUE

The cultural and spiritual characteristics of the Japanese people have emerged from their national history of nearly 20 centuries. This long history reflects the Japanese people's efforts to create and maintain their unique culture. It also reflects the strong influence of foreign cultures. The ancient Chinese and Korean cultures were the first to affect Japan, and their impact on the nation was greatest early in its history. Western cultures have affected the nation impressively during the modern age. The course of their national history has profoundly shaped the ways the Japanese regard themselves and their nation and their relationships with other people.

Three historical interpretations contribute significantly to an understanding of Japan. Each is discussed here as a response to a specific question:
1. How did Buddhism, entering Japan from India through China and Korea, come to assume its unique Japanese character?
2. What are the essential qualities of Japan's traditional "Bushido" way of life?
3. What was the meaning of the Edo era, coming when the world was comparatively stabilized?

Although the Edo era was a period in which Japan was isolated from overseas countries as a result of the closed-door policy, the country continued its economic development. Enduring cultural features of Japan were shaped during this period. Characteristics of the Japanese style were established. This essay discusses aspects of the traditional character of Japan.

Buddhism and Japanese Tradition

Buddhism was introduced into Japan from Korea in the middle of the 6th Century. Initially, this new religion was not welcomed. Buddhism in fact gave rise to a fierce, violent rivalry between the "Soga" clan, advocates of Buddhism, and the "Mononobe" clan, which rejected the alien religious faith. Buddhism eventually triumphed. The imported faith spread throughout the country and eventually influenced almost every facet of the Japanese people's ways of living and thinking.

Imperial Prince Shotoku (574–622) played a very significant role in the establishment of Buddhism in Japan. In his capacity as crown prince and regent, he instituted his widely known "Constitution of 17 Articles." Article I featured a call for "Harmony" as the fundamental principle of national government. Buddhism was defined in Article II as an ultimate truth to which all human beings were to resort. Prince Shotoku hoped that Buddhism would create a peaceful life for all people, eliminating rivalry and strife through universal discussions and cooperation. Certainly, his aspiration may be interpreted as an exercise of the spirit of Buddhism's "compassion." In addition to this leadership, the prince is also credited with having constructed in Nara the Temple of Horyuji, still one of Japan's most prized historical treasures.

During the Nara period (710–783 A.D.), Buddhism assumed the character of a nationalistic faith to uphold Japan's nationhood, rather than the character of a spiritual faith to support and give relief to individuals. Thus, Emperor Shomu (701–756), desiring to ensure the national security then menaced by a succession of serious natural disasters throughout the land, ordered a nationwide drive to produce images of various buddhas and transcripts of various Buddhist sutras. He also completed an ambitious project to have a giant bronze statue of the Vairocana-buddha (the Buddha of Eternally Tranquil Light) cast and sanctified in the Temple of Todaiji which was built at the same time at Nara. Many provincial branches of that temple were built throughout Japan.

Meanwhile, other events transpired. The priest Gyoki (668–749), for example, played a significant role in engineering and construction, taking the lead in canal digging and waterfront building projects. Statues of various other Buddhas were erected and worshipped, including the Buddha of Healing and the Buddha of Mercy and Love. Buddhism in Japan was thus transformed, taking on the double function of serving national security and meeting the realistic day-to-day needs of its adherents.

Several hundred years later, in the Kamakura period (1192–1332 A.D.), Buddhism in Japan recovered its original character as a religious faith for all individuals. The priest Honen (1133–1212) endeavored to turn the prevailing Japanese-style Buddhism into a religious faith for the masses of people. He advocated an absolute belief in the Buddha of Amida, representing compassion and equality, and a faith in the "power of the other," that is, the power of that Buddha in contrast to the power of the self. His disciple, the priest Shinran, claimed that "it was the evil people who were the most ready to be saved" by the inifinite love of the Buddha of Amida. In other words, the more sinful one was, the sharper were one's sense of guilt and urging of conscience to accept the truth of Buddhism. What Shinran preached was that the compassion of the Buddhas was not limited to the priesthood or any other privileged class, as popular belief then held. Rather, it was available to everybody, regardless of occupation and station in life, because the Buddha of Amida dispensed his compassion equally to all those expressing their absolute allegiance to him.

In contrast to such reliance upon the Buddha's power preached by Shinran, the later Chinese-developed and -exported Zen sect of Buddhism called for enlightenment by individual efforts—that is, by one's own spiritual power. The priest Eisai (1141–1215), Japan's Zen pioneer, inaugurated his temple of Eihei in the Province of Echizen—today's Fukui Prefecture. He advocated an extremely stoic practice of Zen meditation, in a motionless sitting position, aloof from all secular desires, including ambition for political power or wealth. He claimed that everybody could attain the enlightenment of Buddhism by such deliberate practice of Zen.

Many Buddhist prelates of the Kamakura period were lofty and single-minded personalities who strove diligently to reconsider the human condition. They attempted to break down the ritualism to which every religious faith is susceptible, and to convert Buddhism into its purest form—that is, a spiritual belief dwelling within individuals. These priests worked zealously for universal realization of the Buddha's compassion in every soul on a perfectly equal basis, and they defied all sorts of persecution of their missionary activities. In their quest for spiritual salvation, most of Japan's "bushi" (samurai) class were converted to Buddhism during the Kamakura period.

Between the Muromachi period (1336–1573 A.D.) and the Edo period (1603–1867 A.D.), Japan's Buddhism tended toward secularization as different Buddhist sects expanded their following and became politically active. In opposition to such a tendency, movements for revival of the basic Buddhist spirit of compassion began to develop and, indeed, persist to the present day.

Bushido in Japanese Culture

During the 10th century, Japan's provincial political security was disrupted and local law and order was thrown into disarray. Each influential farmer felt a pressing need to protect his estate or other property. Each such landowner's large family group was organized into an armed force to fight off invasions and to repress dissident peasants under his control. These circumstances produced Japan's historical social class of warriors or "samurai," also known as the "bushi." These warriors grouped themselves into their own regional "bushi" communities, each centering on the most powerful local samurai.

Between the 10th and 14th Centuries, the "Heishi" and "Genji" clans became the most typical examples of such "bushi" communities. The Heishi clan was predominant at first, having captured the ruling power of Japan from the preceding aristocratic Fujiwara clan. Eventually, the Heishi clan was ruined by its final defeat in the well-known Gen-Pei War.

In 1192, Yoritomo Minamoto, the lord of the Genji clan, inaugurated his feudalistic national government at Kamakura, his clan's home city. For the subsequent 700 years, Japan was subject to the rule of one or another "bushi" clan, though the Emperor and his family maintained status as honored figureheads.

In every campaign of war, Yoritomo secured the signed pledge of every local "bushi" to reply to his mustering call. Every such "bushi" with his own fighting force was known as "gokenin" (clansman-samurai). Yoritomo rewarded every gokenin for answering his mustering call by reconfirming the gokenin's right to continue to own his lands or granting new or additional territory. Each gokenin responded to that benefit by his continuing loyal service. Those master-retainer relationships, based on such benefit and service, are identified as Japan's feudal samurai relationships.

A legendary story, "Hachinoki" (A Potted Bush), illustrates the strength of such lord-retainer relationships. According to legend, Tokiyori Hojo, an executive of the ruling national government at Kamakura, was traveling alone and incognito, in the guise of an itinerant Buddhist priest. He sought to stay overnight at a rundown provincial house during a heavy snowfall. Lacking firewood, the impoverished master of the house was nevertheless so generous to the traveling stranger that he cut up his treasured Bonsai trees and used them to fuel the fireplace. The master of the house identified himself as a former landed samurai who had been unfairly deprived of his territorial land and driven into poverty. "But, nonetheless," he said, "I am keeping my horse and arms in good condition to be ready to rush up to Kamakura in case of an emergency." When

Tokiyori was back in Kamakura, he issued an "emergency" mustering call to gather all henchmen to Kamakura in a rush to test the truth of what that neglected warrior had said. The man was certainly the first to rush up on his undernourished horse. Tokiyori was so impressed by this display of loyalty that he arranged for the man to recover his lost lands, and, moreover, he granted the man an additional estate.

Indeed, the supreme duty of every "bushi" was to be perfectly loyal to his lord. To be more specific, the goal of every "bushi" was to win his battle with every enemy. Therefore, a "bushi" was constantly training in the martial arts without indulging in the luxuries of life. He was educated to be always on the alert against physical attacks by instructive admonitions such as, "Every bushi will have seven enemies on the wait once he steps out of his home." He constantly faced the danger of being attacked anywhere and anytime.

The "bushi" was thus required to be physically and mentally prepared to move in a split second against every attacker and to slash his assailant with his own sword. Such a constant preparedness to fight was not to be relaxed at any moment of his daily life. Ultimately, self-discipline to overcome his own carnal desires was found to be a prerequisite to such a capacity to win every fight with his enemies.

The spirit of the "bushi"—that is, "Bushido"—thus came to be identified as "self-discipline." Every "bushi" strove to control himself, thereby developing a personality worthy of his own self-respect and the esteem of everybody else. This spirit of "bushi" persisted in the Japanese samurai community from the Muromachi to the Edo period.

Japan's Isolation to the Opening of Japan's Door

The "bushi" government of Edo (today's Tokyo) isolated Japan from the world as a consequence of its policy to prohibit propagation of Christianity in the country. It is estimated that early in the 17th century Japanese believers in Christianity numbered 700,000. The Edo authorities, in 1612, intensified their earlier mild suppression of Christians. The repression increased, though met by resistance from Christian believers, and developed steadily into the complete international isolation of Japan by 1639, with a total exclusion of the Portuguese who hitherto had visited Japan. The ban was only slightly eased later, when Dutch and Chinese ships were permitted to trade at the single seaport of Nagasaki under the stern surveillance of the Edo-appointed authorities.

Japan's near total isolation from the world continued for more than two centuries and resulted in the nation's lagging behind Western nations in industrialization and modern progress. Nevertheless, the nation made the most of that period of isolation, improving its feudal system and developing its industries, thereby laying the foundation for its subsequent development into a modern national community.

The government at Edo maintained national order through its central rule and its appointed feudal lords' regional rule. Rigid social class distinctions divided the whole nation, in order of status and respectability, into "bushi," farmer, and townsfolk strata. Social status was inseparably connected with the traditional family system of Japan. Thus, an individual's status passed to his descendants as a natural accompaniment of family heritage. Inherited social status was almost always unchangeable.

Thus, importance was attached to family lineage, and the master of each family had powerful influence over each family member. Among children of a given family, the eldest son, as heir apparent, was the most important of all. Under the prevailing male-dominated system, women were kept in lowly positions within their families. Occupations were also hereditary. Freedom of choice as to means of livelihood was unknown.

The social status of individuals was also subdivided into multiple levels according to family standing. In the "bushi" community, in particular, family standing was very important. Discrimination of individuals because of social status and family level was such a pervasive practice that every individual was expected to act according to his (or her) position in respect to marriage and social relationships, conduct, and daily mode of living.

A clear demarcation between upper and lower status individuals and between masters and servants prevailed throughout Japanese society. Not only the lord and vassals in the "bushi" community, but the original family and its offshoot families in a group of relatives, the parents and children in a family, the husband and wife, the employer and employees in a business house, and the artesan and his apprentices invariably were defined as people in master-and-servant relationships. All underlings were expected to give absolute obedience to their masters.

Meanwhile, the government at Edo and all feudal lords' regional administrations, in their efforts to collect sufficient revenues from land taxes in kind from farmers, encouraged farming techniques to reclaim wasteland and cultivate new paddies to yield larger harvests. Such efforts brought improvement in farming implements and techniques to boost agricultural production. Economic development was not limited to agriculture. Development of cottage industries in textiles, pottery, lacquer ware, and Japanese paper created regional staple products in different parts of the country.

Japan's domestic economy thus expanded. Its regional industrial growth gave rise to many prosperous commercial, waterfront, temple- or shrine-centered, and travel route station communities. Japan's several urban populations swelled as more people left rural areas. By the middle of the 18th Century, Edo registered one million inhabitants (including both the "bushi" and townsfolk classes); Osaka, 380,000 (counting only its predominant townsfolk class); and Kyoto; 350,000 (also counting only its majority townsfolk group).

Japan finally opened its door to international intercourse in 1854 as the result of visits by the United States' Commodore Matthew Calbraith Perry and his naval fleet. However, during the long period of its international isolation, Japan, so to speak, had been silently preparing itself for its emergence into the world's community of nations. Japan rapidly modernized itself after its political renovation during the Meiji Era (1868–1912). However, Japan's traditional culture is not easily changed. Rather, it is inherited in the daily life of the Japanese. Elements of this traditional culture were created during the course of Japanese history over a long period of centuries, many of them having been perfected particularly in the Edo era. Notwithstanding the fact that the closed door policy left Japan behind in the currents of world history, during that entire era Japanese culture was evolving. The contemporary Japanese face the task of preserving that cultural life in a new era, while cooperating with other nations of the international community, and contributing to world peace. These are the important issues which the Japanese must deal with from now on.

REFERENCES

Chuokoronsha. *Nihonnorekishi* [Japan's history]. 26 vols. Chuokoronsha, 1965–67.

Hayashiva, Shinzaburo. *Kinseidentobunkaron* [A study of pre-modern traditional culture]. Sogensha, 1974.

Ishida, Kazuyoshi. *Nihonbunkashigairon* [An introduction to cultural history of Japan]. Yoshikawakobunkan, 1968.

Ishii, Susumu, and Ishimoda, Tadashi. *Chuseiseijishakaishisoshi* [A history of political and social thought in the medieval Japan]. Iwanami, 1972.

Itoh, Shuntaro. *Nihonjin no shakai* [The Japanese society]. Kenkyusha, 1977.

Iwanamikoza. *Nihonrekishi* [The history of Japan]. 26 vols. Iwanami, 1976–78.

Janssen, M.B. *Nihon ni okeru kindaika no mondai* [Issues of modernization in Japan]. Iwanami, 1969.

Nara, Yasuaki. *Nihonbukkyokisokoza* [An introductory course to Japanese Buddhism]. 6 vols. Yuzankaku, 1977.

Saigusa, Mitsuyoshi. *Bukkyoshiso* [Buddhism thought]. 4 vols. Risosha, 1977.

Sansom, G.B. *Sekaishi ni okeru nihon* [Japan in world history]. Iwanami, 1952.

Sansom, G.B. *Seohsekai to nihon* [The western world and Japan]. Chikuma, 1974.

Toyota, Takeshi and Hall, Johnson. *Muromachi jidai, sono shakai to bunka* [Muromachi era—its society and culture]. Yoshikawakobunkan, 1976.

CHAPTER THREE

Japan's Economy: Strong but Weak

YOSHIRO KURISAKA

Japan is a small island country in the Far East, isolated half a world away from the Western industrial countries. It is not quite as large as California, but supports a densely packed population nearly half as large as that of the United States.

Natural resources are far from sufficient. The country is almost entirely dependent on foreign sources for oil, iron ore, nickel, and copper. In food supplies too, Japan has a deficit of 60 percent, and is self-sufficient only in rice. Its dependence on international trade for its very survival makes the nation extremely vulnerable to major international disruptions. If a war broke out and Japan's shipping lanes were blocked, the country would be all but strangled.

Japan has become an economic giant, ranking second in the free world. But it can only remain a great nation in peacetime. Japan is, indeed, a "strong but weak" nation.

Compact Economy

Japan has a racially homogeneous population of 118 million on its small sea-enclosed land. Roughly half of its inhabitants live on the 350-mile strip of Pacific coast that extends westward from Tokyo to the Osaka region. This concentration has been instrumental in shaping a highly cost-efficient market where transportation expenses are no significant burden on consumption or production. A surprising uniformity in consumer response stems largely from Japan's uniform society. Coupled with the high purchasing power of the people, this standardized consumption pattern has been conducive to the emergence of a compact economy that makes the mass-production and mass-consumption pattern fit ideally into the small country.

The oceans surrounding Japan provide a far more economical means for the massive transportation of goods than would highways or railroads. Distant shipments of oil, coal, iron ore, and grain by giant seagoing vessels cost barely one-tenth as much as overland transportation of the same materials. In Japan, modern steel mills and other heavy industrial complexes are invariably located by the sea, many on land reclaimed from the ocean. Transportation costs thus are eased. This gives Japanese industry a great advantage over the United States, the Soviet Union, and China. Japan is thus linked with world markets by the efficient "highways" of the oceans.

The surrounding oceans also provide Japan with another strategic advantage. Today, as in the past, the sea serves an ideal defense line. Therefore, defense expenditures of the island nation can be kept relatively low, compared with those of nations on a continent, especially nations bordered by a threatening superpower such as the Soviet Union.

The compact economy of Japan also facilitates the maximum utilization of natural resources. A general lack of space on the overcrowded land creates a market for compact products—from home to vehicle to air conditioner—and the result is an exceptionally economical use of natural resources and energy. When the recent oil crisis forced increased efforts to conserve energy, Japan's traditional stress on frugality came into full play. The more efficient use of its compact goods made the nation unexpectedly resilient in the oil crunch. There were eager responses from industry, as well, and general efforts proved so successful that the energy requirement per unit of production has been reduced by more than 10 percent. The advent of the age of energy conservation has helped push Japanese automobiles into the world spotlight. The global popularity of Japanese cars is not so surprising when one considers that they are built to meet the needs of the compact economy at home.

Pollution and other environmental disruptions are an inevitable by-product of the rapid economic growth of the crowded nation of Japan. The government has attacked the problem with the world's most rigid anti-pollution regulations. To comply with these, Japanese industry has developed sophisticated pollution control systems for steel mills, power plants, auto factories, and other facilities. Today, not a single factory chimney in Japan is belching smoke.

The instinct for survival was a major driving force behind Japan's phenomenal restoration after the devastation of World War II. Its lack of natural resources spurred the more recent technological advances. The dynamic growth of the Japanese economy has been motivated by the proverbial dictum that "necessity is the mother of invention."

Catching Up with the Western World

When Japan was about to make its delayed start toward building a modern nation following the Meiji Restoration of 1868, one encouraging factor was the existence of a strong national consensus in favor of modernization. The consensus was an important product of the modern education system that was taking firm hold across the nation. It was also reinforced by the traditional Confucian ethic emphasizing hard work and loyalty to superiors. For national survival and development, the government decided to build a strong nation, equal to the Western powers, through the aggressive introduction of cultural achievements, scientific knowledge, and technical skills from the West. The public was indoctrinated to embrace the national aspiration of "catching up with the Western world," and soon the newly coined phrase "Japanese spirit with Western knowledge" began to illustrate the ideal image of the modern Japanese.

Japan's modernization, however, was not attained without major setbacks. Too much confidence in what it had achieved led the nation to disastrous defeat in World War II. Its aspiration to catch up with the West remained very much alive, however, and provided a significant prop to the swift economic revival and ensuing expansion which has occurred in the past two decades.

The national emphasis on education in Japan has given rise to stiff competition among students aspiring ultimately to pass the entrance examinations of the University of Tokyo and other "blue-ribbon" universities. Hard work in pre-university schooling helps foster the spirit of discipline and patience in students, along with that of competitiveness. With a military career no longer attractive in today's peace-oriented Japan, elite university graduates enter business in large numbers, adding to the social prestige of big companies.

Forced to make a shaky start in the early postwar years, Japanese business engaged in keen competition for an increased market share and brand-name prestige. Playing central roles were junior executives whose harsh wartime experiences honed their skills in building well-organized businesses. The wholesale introduction of advanced Western technologies did not merely upgrade the technological level of Japanese companies, but it also ensured easier access to the Western world. Developments quickly led to increased Japanese enthusiasm to tap Western markets.

In Japan, the most grueling competition has taken place among automobile, electrical appliance, and camera manufacturers. The fact that the quality of their products is now recognized around the world demonstrates that competition was a significant element in the nation's rapid economic growth.

Bottom-to-Top Decision-Making

One common impression among Western businessmen is that Japanese business is rather slow in making decisions but quick to put decisions into practice. Many also complain that one cannot be sure who makes the decisions.

In Western companies, an unmistakable process of decision-making is observable. It gives more power to the man of higher position, forming a leadership ladder from chairman down to president, executive, and manager. While this system facilitates instant decision-making, it also has its drawbacks. Quite frequently, subordinates are rather slow in carrying out unfamiliar decisions or implementing new projects handed to them by their superiors.

This top-to-bottom pattern of decision-making stands in sharp contrast to the Japanese system, which moves from bottom to top. In Japan, top corporate executives naturally have great power. Any major business transaction, projection, or idea of top executives, however, is first referred to members of the staff at the bottom, and decision-making starts its way up with almost bureaucratic formality. When the matter at hand is cleared by the bottom group, often with some revision, it is forwarded to men in higher positions step by step until it reaches the top level for final decision-making. This process is called the "ringi" system. Time-consuming though it may appear, the system makes the staff fully familiar with a proposal and capable of carrying it out rapidly.

In working out a major corporate policy, all that the chairman or president does is explain to his staff where the company stands and where it should go. The operational policy draft comes up gradually from the bottom. Junior executives in Japan generally have a strong say in decision-making, holding the actual reins of the company. Behind the smooth functioning of this decision-making system lies the full reliance of the chairman and president on their subordinates. This reliance is a product of their philosophy that a company is a community of people with common interests. Fierce competition with other companies often makes top executives preoccupied with the long-term growth prospects of their company or its importance in the life of the nation rather than immediate profits. These far-sighted objectives require the cooperation of all employees, and the maximum utilization of the bottom-to-top decision-making system works well for these purposes. The attitude of Japanese top executives, indeed, differs radically from the American management emphasis on corporate stability to please the shareholders.

Large Crowded Offices

Western businessmen accustomed to individual offices would be surprised if they visited a Japanese company and found a large number of workers—often as many as 50 or more—sitting at rows of desks in a huge office. These workers would include section chiefs, department managers, and often executives. This all-in-one-office system would be extraordinary by Western standards. In fact, an experiment at an Italian bank using such a formula ended in failure because of the many complaints about disruptive noise arising from many conversations.

The Japanese system, however, is not without benefits. Being in a large room together, workers learn what is going on in different sections through overhearing conversations or picking up unanswered telephones at adjacent desks. Noise is certainly a nuisance, but the disadvantages are more than offset by the benefit of improved communication among superiors, subordinates, and workers.

There is a traditional love of group interaction among the Japanese people, as demonstrated by the close bond of family and relatives or the frequent gatherings of alumni many years after graduation. The importance of the group is striking among office workers as well, even after work. A superior will take some of his subordinates to a neighborhood drinking place to express his personal thanks for their work that day. When colleagues socialize, they often commiserate, complaining about their superiors while having a few drinks. These after-hours get-togethers are largely recreational, but quite frequently are work-oriented, as well.

Not surprisingly, there is less individual identity in a large office. Occasionally, hard work required of some workers has a cumulative effect of creating a peculiar office environment—one in which other workers feel psychological pressure to do, or pretend to do, less urgent tasks after normal work hours. This kind of situation may be responsible in part for the popular Western myth about the hard-working Japanese. Even if the work intensity in a large office is not as great as it may appear, working in a large group benefits communication and the individual sense of participation and involvement. One undeniable fact, however, is that workers, fearful of possible alienation, must stifle much of their individuality on and away from the job.

Lifelong Competition

While the common strategy of Western management during a business slump is to lay off workers, Japanese management usually continues to retain all workers in accordance with the distinctive Japanese system of lifetime employment. The system is accepted as a matter of course, and no employment contract stipulates such job security. Except in the case of most small businesses, workers are generally assured of employment until the company's fixed retirement age. Behind the system is the Japanese concept that employment means totally belonging to the company, which is a striking contrast to the Western concept that laborers simply receive monetary reward in return for specific individual skills. One side benefit of this Japanese system is an individual's strong sense of loyalty to the company. This loyalty is illustrated by the phrase, "my company," frequently used by Japanese workers. Since individual skills are of less significance, versatile and cooperative employees are preferred to specialists—even ones holding doctorates—in the selection of new personnel. The young recruits are then educated to be skilled workers as desired by the company through on-the-job training.

Dismissal in Japan is the last resort during a recession. Surplus labor is shifted to other departments of the company or sent to affiliated enterprises. Further reversals of business are coped with by reducing or simply suspending the recruitment of new workers. At the height of a crisis, voluntary early retirement is encouraged with the reward of extra retirement allowances. While management pressure on workers for early retirement is not rare, the company sometimes is lenient enough to reemploy some of them on a temporary basis.

When the recent oil crisis dealt a severe blow to the nation's shipbuilding industry, one popular practice was to shift workers from dockyards to machinery production lines being operated by many shipbuilders. One company had the great bulk of its shipyard workers employed by an affiliated automaker. Japan's largest enterprise, Nippon Steel Corporation, went through its business hardships by scaling down its new employment program during the crisis years, in tandem with a wholesale modernization of production facilities. Eight years of its efforts were rewarded by a reduction in personnel from 85,000 to 75,000 with no impact on production.

Coupled with lifetime employment, a stress on seniority is characteristic of Japanese business. Based perhaps on Confucian philosophy, the seniority system offers higher company standing and more salary to older workers who are believed to be more valuable than younger ones. This system has no parallel in other industrial countries, where wage scales are rather staid, essentially determined by craft.

The permanent employment and seniority systems seemingly are a comfortable assurance of slow, but steady ascent up the ladder of promotion and increased pay. One depressing factor, however, is the possible erosion of the spirit of challenge. In fact, many promising young workers are found to be discouraged by the absence of immediate incentives. Working in a Japanese company is not without its drawbacks. Many employees are subject to frequent changes in work assignment which often mean transferring to a different office. Each shift causes no small strain psychologically and physically, and the hardship is beyond description if one has to endure moving to distant branch offices ten or more times during a career. Under the seniority system, surprise promotion is something quite rare, because of its discouraging impact on other workers of the same class and level. Aspiring to move only a step ahead of their colleagues, workers engage in severe competition which often lasts until retirement. The operation of a Japanese company, indeed, rests on a subtle balance between the keen competition among colleagues and the paternalistic interest of management in employees, weighted by in-service training.

Company-Wide Union

The basic unit of Japan's labor union movement is the company-wide union encompassing all the workers of a company—a striking contrast to the craft union in Western countries. Bargaining over wages and work conditions is conducted between management and labor of each company, and the sense of belonging to the same institution is reflected in their cooperative attitudes. As a result, fewer man-days are lost in strikes or other labor disputes than in other industrial countries, except for the shipping and aviation sectors. In a sense, it was the cooperation of the unions that provided a significant momentum for the economic rise of Japan.

The peculiar nature of the nation's labor unions is built on the traditional sense of paternalism which still lingers within each company—a tribute to the brief history of confrontation between management and labor in Japan. The wartime suspension of labor movements helped it to survive, and, during most of the early postwar years, confrontation had to give way to cooperation in order to prevent companies from collapsing. Unmistakably, the union is a product of the group-oriented attitude that has long characterized Japanese society. Such unions are quite foreign to Western society.

Through company-wide unions, more than 30 percent of the Japanese labor force is organized—a rate much higher than in the United States, where less than 25 percent is organized. The individual unions gather to form national organizations which are different from industry to industry, and above them are such overarching federations as SOHYO and DOMEI.[1] These federations are strong political pressure groups with a commanding influence on their numerous member unions through issuance of bargaining guidelines. The ultimate decision-making authority, however, belongs to the individual enterprise unions.

Under the company-wide union system, management and labor are in the same boat. Increased corporate earnings more or less result in increased wages and other allowances, as well as in better work conditions. Bankruptcy spells doom for both management and labor. It is no wonder then that the union takes a particular interest in how the company is faring economically. Since workers are not organized by craft, they put up less resistance to job transfers within the company. The introduction of modern facilities is seldom opposed because possible labor surplus will not lead directly to dismissal under the permanent employment system. Workers even welcome such technological advances, which they know will add to the productivity and earnings of their company. They are also happy to see their company outrun its rivals and gain higher social prestige.

Many corporate executives in charge of labor relations are former union leaders. Aspiring young workers are willing to engage in union activities, encouraged by the fact that knowledge about business and labor management acquired through union work often promises a successful career. The close human link between management and labor facilitates communication at the bargaining table and helps a great deal to lead many labor disputes to peaceful and prompt set-

---

[1]SOHYO is the General Council of Trade Unions of Japan; DOMEI is the Japanese Confederation of Labor.

tlement. Japanese management usually can depend on the union to support corporate growth. This distinctive spirit of cooperation has made possible Japan's remarkable productivity rise and quality control.

Productivity and Quality Control

Increased productivity and improved quality control are important slogans at most Japanese factories. These concepts are not of Japanese invention, but have been adopted from Western countries. What has made Japan exceptionally successful in these areas is the great enthusiasm which the Japanese have displayed in pursuing the ultimate in these concepts. One shining results is the global popularity of such high-quality Japanese products as automobiles, cameras, and electronic appliances.

Over the past 20 years, the volume of Japanese production per man-hour has risen roughly three times as fast as that in the United States. Credit for this development belongs in large part to the unreserved business spendings in new plant and equipment which are primarily intended for corporate survival amidst bitter competition.

At the end of the war, all of Japan's factories were destroyed. In order to survive economically, Japan had to build new factories capable of manufacturing exportable products at minimum cost so that the nation could buy imports of food and natural resources. In the ensuing years, heavy investment in more sophisticated factories continued, with the additional aim of increased productivity, which was supported by the active introduction of superior Western technologies. Traditionally, the Japanese have a propensity to save, and individual savings were readily available as investment funds through the banking system. Supplying large capital funds often involved risk, but banks were more concerned about the long-term prospects for their client companies and their competitive posture than they were of losing some monies.

These investment efforts have been rewarded amply. Of the 22 most up-to-date steel mills operating in the world in 1980, 14 were in Japan while none was in the United States. In the auto industry, Japan had roughly 10,000 robots in operation in the same year, as reported by *Time* magazine, compared with 3,000 in the United States. Investment in one industry has multiplied the volume of investment in related industries, and this chain reaction has set the pace for the dazzling economic growth of Japan.

During the 1950s, Japanese manufacturers enthusiastically embraced the statistical approach to effective quality control recommended by Dr. W. Edwards Deming of the United States. Soon, his method was in widespred use—and each year in Japan, a nationwide quality control contest is held. The winning company is presented with the coveted Deming Medal, one of the highest honors in Japanese industry.

Most factories now maintain numerous quality control groups. Called "QC circles," each is composed of 10 or fewer employees. These groups are made up of production line workers striving to enhance and develop the quality of their products. Japan's achievement in quality control has outshone its teacher, the United States. Much credit undoubtedly belongs to the great efforts of industry as a whole, but a result of this brilliance would never have been attained without steady competition among manufacturers and the particularly discriminating Japanese consumers who demand unfailing quality at a reasonable price.

In carrying out quality control and zero-defect compaigns, many companies maintain a system that encourages proposals for improved credibility of products from QC circles and individual workers. The employee proposal system at the Toyota Motor factories offers monetary rewards for excellent suggestions, and there are some 500,000 proposals received each year, averaging 10 for each worker. This system also produces an important side benefit—that is, the increased sense of involvement of all employees.

Future Problems

The phenomenal economic rise of Japan has been called "the Japanese miracle." Additionally, its surefooted economic performance after the oil crisis of the 1970s earned it another description—"the gold medalist in the economic Olympics."

But Japan faces many challenging problems requiring solutions immediately or in the years ahead. One is its trade disputes with the outside world. Japan's rapidly rising exports have produced growing protectionist sentiments and moves to restrict imports of Japanese goods. One possible remedy is to increase overseas investment to start local production, but this move will be accompanied by sizable downward pressure on employment at home. For the automobile and home appliance industries, the problem is magnified by a possible sales letdown, with consumer demand near its peak both at home and abroad. Clearly, more efforts will be required to develop attractive new products. The rapid rise of newly industrialized countries is likely to push Japanese industry farther toward more sophisticated, high-technology areas. Japan also will be required to make increased efforts to secure stable supplies of energy and other natural resources, review its national security policy, and deal with expanding economic commitments in developing countries.

Further in the future, the aging of the labor force will emerge as another serious problem. By the year 2000, people over 65 years of age are expected to constitute no less than 15 percent of the entire population. Efforts to create job opportunities for the elderly and guarantee a livelihood for them will become a heavier burden on business and government. Young workers may face difficulties as well. Having grown up in an affluent society, they may well display less enthusiasm for the difficult, disciplined and demanding work that has made possible the nation's economic rise. Also emerging in Japan's male-dominated business society are women who are dissatisfied with the status quo. Demanding more job opportunities, women are likely to have a strong impact on the nation's working habits and conditions in years to come.

The distinctive operational attitudes of Japanese business are shaped in large part by the specific natural environment and historical heritage of the nation. While immediate change in the attitudes seem unlikely, their evolution into different patterns will be inevitable 10 or 20 years from now. Harvard University professor Ezra Vogel emphasizes the superiority of the Japanese economy and society in his work entitled *Japan as Number One*. Many Japanese analysts, on the other hand, hold a different opinion. They point out that Japan's heavy dependence on the natural resources and markets of the outside world makes the nation particularly susceptible to international disturbances. The organizational style of its economy will also undergo substantial changes in the long run. With these challenging problems in mind, many analysts insist that the Japanese economy and society would be better described as "Japan as if Number One."

After all, Japan's economy is very easily influenced by overseas market fluctuations, and international political affairs. Only a limited range of options seems to be available to Japan to decide its own future.

REFERENCES

Hodgson, James Day, "The American Business Scene: A Few Thoughts for Japanese Managers," *Speaking of Japan*, Jan., 1981, published by Keizai Koho Center, pp. 25–29.

Kamijo, Toshiaki, "Japan's Paradox," *Economic Eye*, Sept., 1980, published by Keizai Koho Center, pp. 3–5.

Karatsu, Hajime, "Quality Control: The Japanese Approach," *Economic Eye*, Dec., 1981, pp. 29–32.

Kurisaka, Yoshiro, "Running into Difficulties," *Speaking of Japan*, May, 1982, pp. 12–16.

Mansfield, Mike, "Our U.S.-Japan Relationship," *Speaking of Japan*, July, 1981, pp. 1–4.

Momoi, Makoto, "The Road to Energy Security," *Economic Eye*, Dec., 1980, pp. 9–14.

Nagamori, Yuichi, "People and Robots: Working Together," *Economic Eye*, Sept., 1982, pp. 27–32.

Shimizu, Yoshihei, "Japanese Sense of Labor," *Speaking of Japan*, March, 1981, pp. 22–25.

Shinotsuka, Eiko, "Women in the Labor Force," *Economic Eye*, Sept., 1982, pp. 22–26.

CHAPTER FOUR

The Role of Women
in Japanese Society

YORIKO MEGURO

In contrast with the high visibility of Japan's economic development in the past three decades, women in Japanese society have remained invisible. Nevertheless, the social environments of women have been changing, and some of the changes have influenced women's status and role considerably.

The most fundamental change affecting women in the post-World War II period has occurred in Japanese law. The new Constitution mandated an egalitarian principle which emancipated women from their submissive status to men in various spheres of life. New, equal rights were promised to women in such areas as education, family life, and work.

A changing industrial structure invited women to join the labor market, but in discriminatory ways. Although the number of unpaid family workers has decreased gradually, many women continue to make economic contributions as non-employees.

The rise in the level of the nation's education has been remarkable. Higher education in Japan, however, has not functioned in such a way as to influence women's work and career orientation. It would be a fair statement that the Japanese educational system has functioned to reinforce the traditional sex-based division of labor in society.

Freedom in the selection of marriage partners has become a natural right for the younger generations. Marriage, however, continues to mean a support system for women, and women's lives depend to a great extent on their husbands.

Some demographic changes such as the lengthening of life expectancy and the decline in fertility have begun to influence the traditional life cycles of the Japanese people. The emerging pattern suggests that both men and women must face an entirely new phase of life, as individuals live longer with yet ambiguous role expectations.

Historical Background and Cultural Constraints

Before World War II, division of labor by sex was legally defined as a relationship between the ruler and the ruled. The Japanese sex-role ideology was and continued to be rooted in the feudal ideology of the warrior class, which became institutionalized in Japanese society during the Meiji period. This reinforcement of feudal ideology was, in fact, paradoxical. During the Meiji era, the early phase of Japan's modernization process, the Samurai ideology of female submission to the male became the rule even among the common people. The Meiji modernization, one may see, played a retrogressive role in Japanese male-female relationships.

Education is often one of the factors correlated with modernization. The Meiji government emphasized the importance of educating both men and women as early as 1872, only five years after the establishment of the modern regime. This policy, however, was rooted in the belief that women should be educated to become "wise mothers" so as to raise good citizens.[1] This idea held that all women were to become "mothers" in order to serve the state. Emori Ueki, a well-known social reformer of the Meiji era, presented a plan in 1887 for setting up middle schools for girls. He claimed that it was essential to reform education for girls in order to produce mothers who might become good educators in the home and with innovative ideas foster future social reformers.[2] The government and liberal social reformers, such as Ueki, were all interested in educating women solely in view of their role as nurturers of the future generation. This basic notion of education for women to make them "good and wise mothers," serving the state's interest, has survived to the present day.

One striking aspect of modernization in Japan is found in the family system. Under the pre-World War II civil code, the basic family system called the *Ie* was considered ideal. The *Ie* system was based on Confucian ethics which prevailed in the Samurai ruling class in the pre-modern (Tokugawa) period. Legalized by the Meiji government, this institution became the basis for controlling the

---

[1] Kuni Nakajima, "Meiji Kokka to Bosei," a report presented at a meeting on women's studies, Tokyo, July 18, 1978.

[2] Ibid.

Japanese people. The *Ie*, stated simply, was a patriarchal and patrilineal system under which the rule of primogeniture operated. The family head ideally was the male, and he was the official representative of the family unit before he was an individual husband or father. The most important task of the household head was the lineal continuity of the family and expansion of the family property. Under this system, women were submissive to the male head. The major task expected of the wife was to procreate and to socialize the family successor. Marriage was institutionalized to support the ideology of family continuity.

The majority of prewar families engaged in farming, and the bride was a useful and often essential new laborer on the family farm. She was also a childbearer. Socialization of her children was often placed in the hands of her mother-in-law. For the bride, marriage meant her entrance into the existing household comprising the groom's family and the subsequent assumption of the lowest position in the household. This development was common for every bride regardless of her husband's occupation and status. To compensate for the lack of affection in her relations with her husband, she developed intimate relationships with her children. They were her possessions, and the irreplaceable mother-child relation in the family persisted.

Women's Status and Role in Changing Japan

As a basis for understanding the changing role and status of women in Japan, a description is needed of the general trends which Japan has experienced in the post-World War II period. Industrialization and democratization are the themes underlying all of these changes. In relation to the family and kinship systems, which are the most confining variables determining women's status, the disorganization of the corporate kin group (Dozoku) and the shrinking of the family size have been major issues. A precipitous decline in the mean household size from 4.97 to 3.69 occurred between 1955 and 1970. Household size continued to fall to 3.48 in 1975. The legal negation of the *Ie* ideology, together with demographic and social change, brought about a remarkable increase of conjugal families. Today, of the households composed of more than two kin members, three-fourths take the form of the nuclear family (see Table 1). The rapid and steady increase of the nuclear family in the last 20 years is a reflection of changing family ideology from the *Ie* to the egalitarian conjugal family. This ideology was introduced and supported by the postwar Code. Marriage has become increasingly a personal matter instead of an alliance between families.

Table 1.   Changing Proportions of the Conjugal Family, (By Percentage)

Year	1920	1955	1960	1965	1970	1975
Proportion	57.5	62.0	63.4	68.2	71.3	74.3

Sources: For 1920–1970, K. Morioka, ed., *Shin Kazoku Kankeigaku: (A New Approach to Family Relations)* 1974: 3, for 1975, the Census of Japan.

Table 2.   Wife's Age at Important Events in Family History

	Wife's Age		Duration of Interval (in number of years)	
	1930	1950	1930	1950
A Marriage	22.2	23.0	1.2	1.9
B Birth of 1st Child	23.4	24.9	13.5	3.1
C Birth of Last Child	36.9	28.0	12.0	22.4
D Marriage of 1st Child				
Female	47.4	48.9		
Male	50.4	51.9	13.5	3.1
E Marriage of Last Child				
Female	60.9	52.0		
Male	63.9	55.0	1.6	14.5
F Death of Husband	64.0	68.0	7.0	7.0
G Death of Wife	71.0	75.0		

Source: K. Morioka, *Kazoku Shukiron: (Family Life Cycle)* 1973: 121.

Another important demographic change has been observed in the pattern of women's lives which is comparable to changes occurring in Western industrialized societies. Cohort studies provide a clear indication that the patterns of the family life cycle in two age groups, those married in 1930 and those in 1950, are considerably different (see Table 2). The most outstanding difference between the two is in the length of what might be called the "post-parental" stage. The prolongation of that stage for the 1950 group is caused by the decrease in the number of the family's children and also by longer life expectancy. Another important difference is in a women's age at the birth of her last child. The women in the 1950 cohort would have become relatively free from child-rearing in their mid-thirties and they would cease to hold the mother role in their early fifties. Having the longest life expectancy in the world (77.95 years in 1977), a Japanese woman has 25 to 30 years to live as an individual seeking identity other than as a wife and mother. This is an entirely new experience in Japanese history.

Besides these demographic changes which affect women's status, other notable changes may be identified. Theoretically, these should contribute to an increase in women's power in the family and society. Legalization of equality between sexes probably was the most fundamental change in the postwar period. The new Civil Code of 1948 renounced women's subordination to the men in their family life, namely the father, the husband and the son. The new egalitarian Constitution promised basic human rights and outlawed discrimination based on sex, genealogy, faith, and other individual attributes.

Equal opportunity to receive formal education has encouraged women to continue their education beyond compulsory schooling. In 1975, about 32 percent of women in the applicable age group entered institutions of higher education compared to 44 percent of men; in 1960, on the other hand, less than 6 percent of women and 15 percent of men continued into higher education. Although the policy of equal education for men and women is maintained, the government appears to have emphasized a sex-based curriculum. The Meiji ideology supporting education of women to create good wives and wise mothers underlies the ongoing policy in the formal education of women. This sex-based education socially defines women's roles as homemakers or as inferior members of the labor force, mapping out both lower educational opportunities and lower occupational opportunities for women than for men. College education for women is often considered an extension of preparatory training for good marriage. Sex typing of academic fields is rather clear-cut, and the majority of women going to higher educational institutions are in women's junior colleges.

The Meaning of Work and the Housewife Role

As in many societies, Japanese women have worked throughout their national history mostly on family farms and in family businesses. Only during the past few decades, however, have there been significant numbers of women employed outside the home. Today, out of 22 million working women, 14 million are employed, and they constitute about one-third of the total labor force (see Table 3). The growing shortage of the young labor supply, caused by the rise in the level of education and the drop in the birth rate, enabled women to enter the labor market, particularly in the 1960s when Japan experienced a remarkably high rate of economic growth. Women themselves were more readily available for work due to

Table 3.   Number of Employed Workers and the Proportion of Women, (Numbers in 10 Thousand)

Year	Number of Employed Workers Male	Number of Employed Workers Female	Percent of Women in the Total Employed Force	Number of Employed Workers Total
1955	1,247	531	29.9	1,778
1960	1,632	738	31.1	2,370
1965	1,963	913	31.7	2,876
1970	2,210	1,096	33.2	3,306
1971	2,290	1,116	32.8	3,406
1972	2,332	1,120	32.4	3,452
1973	2,408	1,186	33.0	3,595
1974	2,440	1,171	32.4	3,610
1975	2,479	1,167	32.0	3,646
1976	2,509	1,203	32.4	3,712
1977	2,518	1,251	33.2	3,709
1978	2,519	1,280	33.7	3,799
1979	2,566	1,310	33.8	3,876
1980	2,617	1,354	34.1	3,971
1981	2,646	1,391	34.5	4,037

Sources: Women's and Minors' Bureau, Ministry of Labor, *Fujin Rodo no Jitsujo,* 1975–82.
How to read: In 1981, there were 13,910,000 employed female workers.

Table 4.   Employed Women by Marital Status, (Numbers in 10 Thousand)

Year	Single	Married	Separated/ Divorced	Total
1962	456(59.4%)	225(29.3%)	87(11.3%)	769(100.0%)
1965	466(54.2)	300(34.9)	94(10.9)	860(100.0)
1970	524(48.3)	450(41.4)	112(10.3)	1,086(100.0)
1971	514(46.3)	479(43.2)	116(10.5)	1,109(100.0)
1972	483(43.4)	513(46.1)	116(10.4)	1,113(100.0)
1973	482(40.9)	570(48.3)	126(10.7)	1,179(100.0)
1974	456(39.2)	582(50.0)	124(10.7)	1,163(100.0)
1975	440(38.0)	595(51.3)	125(10.8)	1,184(100.0)
1976	428(35.8)	635(53.1)	131(11.0)	1,203(100.0)
1977	434(34.9)	677(54.5)	132(10.6)	1,242(100.0)
1978	436(34.3)	704(55.4)	131(10.3)	1,271(100.0)
1979	432(33.2)	737(56.7)	132(10.2)	1,300(100.0)
1980	437(32.5)	772(57.4)	135(10.0)	1,345(100.0)
1981	443(32.1)	802(58.0)	136(9.8)	1,382(100.0)

Sources: Women's and Minors' Bureau, Ministry of Labor. *Jufin Roko no Jitsujo,* 1975–82.
How to read: In 1981, there were 4,430,000 employed single women, comprising 32.1% of all employed women.

higher education, which encouraged them to "make observations of societal activities" in the time before they were married and in time free from housework.

Most Japanese employed women have been young and single, but more married and older women are working today than ever before (see Table 4). In 1955, 69 percent of employed women were below 30 years of age and 65 percent were single; in 1974, 56 percent were 30 years old or over and only 39 percent were single. The average age of working women has increased from 25.4 in 1954 to 32.5 in 1974.[3]

Gainful employment has been one of the major factors contributing to the emancipation of women in the Western world. How has it, then, affected the status of women in Japan? Japanese women have participated significantly in the economic activities of the nation, but their compensation has not been commensurate with their contributions. This situation is due in part to some unique features of the Japanese occupational structure. On the other hand, it is also a phenomenon universally observed throughout the world. The income and the retirement systems illustrate the problem women face in the Japanese culture. The ratio of men's salaries to women's has narrowed between 1960 and 1974 from 100:43 to 100:54, but women's average salaries are still less than 60 percent of men's. The low pay for women's work is due to the pattern of sexual steretyping in the occupational structure, with women concentrated in low-paying jobs. Another barrier for Japanese women is related to the lifetime employment system. According to the seniority principle, the longer one works for an employer, the more one is paid. Women usually stay on the job for fewer years than men. Consequently, under the system, they are paid less than men.

The salary gap between the sexes exists regardless of educational backgrounds. A man would get a higher salary than a woman if he had the same amount of education. Public servants and school teachers are among the few exceptions, but the limited advancement opportunities for women result in the widening gap between men and women in the later stages of their careers.

Sex-based retirement policies have been developed by a considerable number of firms. These commonly establish an earlier retirement age for women than for men. In 1975, 2.5 percent of all firms surveyed had a policy of *not* continuing the employment of women who were 35 years old or older.[4] With the increase in the number of working women in recent years and, particularly, since the United Nations proclaimed 1975 as International Women's Year, suits have been filed in courts by women who were forced to leave

---

[3]Women's and Minors' Bureau, *Fujin Rodo no Jitsujo* (Tokyo: Ministry of Labor, 1975), p. 60.

[4]Ibid, p. 74.

their work because of their employer's sex-differentiated retirement policies. The Ministry of Labor has gradually responded to the changing international view of women's work by "advising" employers to abolish sex-segregating retirement policies.

According to the most recent statistics published by the Women's and Minors' Bureau, more married women (67.8 percent of all employed women) are currently employed than ever before. The increase in the number of temporary workers has contributed to the overall increase of women's employment. As in the past, women are used as the safety valve in the management of a fluctuating economy. Middle-aged and married women enter the labor market primarily as part-time workers whose working conditions fall below the level of full-time workers. Women in the most reproductive years (between the ages of 20 and 34) have constituted most of these part-time workers, but an increasing proportion of those in the post-child-rearing period (age 35 and over) have also entered the job market as part-time workers. This situation may be interpreted as a possible trend; apparently, more married women are willing to enter the job market while maintaining their roles as housewives.

When middle-aged married women wish to take full-time jobs, they face serious difficulties in finding openings. Three reasons appear to account for their difficulty. First is Japan's lifetime employment system which does not readily welcome those in the older age brackets as novice employees. The second reason is the required retraining of housewives who have spent a number of years in isolation from the working world. The third reason, closely related to the second, is the sex-role ideology emphasizing home-making as the primary role of women.

If it is true for most Japanese women that their primary responsibility is in the home, why are more women working today than ever before? Many surveys have discovered that financial rewards are the major motivation for women's participation in the labor market.[5]

Working women generally have not been career oriented. More than half of all women who left their jobs in 1974 did so because of marriage and childbirth.[6] Although more women retire from work upon marriage than upon the birth of a child, child-care is the most serious problem facing working women. Unlike women in many Western countries, Japanese women rely heavily on grandmothers to care for children. Women who do not live with or near the

---

[5]See, for example, a survey by N H K, 1975, and one by National Institute for Vocational Research, 1976.

[6]Prime Minister's Office, *Fujin no Genjo to Shisaku* (Tokyo: Gyosei, 1978), p. 81.

grandmother must rely on public and private nursery schools which are still woefully inadequate to meet the need. Husbands are rarely available as babysitters both because they lack the time and because of societal sex-role expectations. Japan's sex-role ideology rests on a deeply embedded notion of "motherhood." Whatever interferes with motherhood becomes the target of criticism, and, thus, those working instead of providing personal child-care tend to feel a sharp sense of guilt. Many career-oriented women abandon their careers for this reason, and many more happily quit working upon marriage or childbirth to fulfill their traditional role. Systems of maternity leave have been discussed with increasing seriousness, but paternity leave is as yet unconsidered by the great majority of firms.

Because of the prevalent norm regarding the division of labor by sex and women's consequent unpreparedness for work, a heavy concentration of women in the occupations with low prestige and pay is observed. A gradual increase of women in more rewarding occupations is seen as leading to the elevation of their status in society.

Conclusion

Japanese society clearly defines sex-segregated roles. Women have little choice in this definition. The priority of the housewife's role overrides all other roles even when those roles constitute important dimensions in a woman's life. The lack of decision-making leaves no room for them to be confused, but it confines them to a state of dependence on others—primarily male family members. Some claim that Japanese women enjoy autonomy in the home. Such autonomy without economic independence, however, denies autonomy to a woman as a social individual. Her life is controlled by the one who provides her financial support. The autonomy that a Japanese woman enjoys within the family exists as long as she maintains peaceful relationships with her provider.

Women have participated in various sectors of social life in Japan. After their suffrage was gained in 1945, women's voting rate gradually increased, and today it exceeds men's. Female representatives in both national and local governmental units, however, still make up a negligible portion of that male-dominated world.

Whether in public service, academia, or mass media, actively participating women are few in number and they are not invited into the decision-making circles. These women, furthermore, tend to believe, to varying degrees, that any strides toward true equality between men and women must be made without disturbing the traditional notion of the woman's "natural" role of housewife. Gradual permeation of new ideologies of equality and of a conjugal family system should provide career-seeking women with many more opportunities and alternative life-styles. Yet, women seem to cling to child-rearing as their last sanctuary. The basis of women's personal identity, in the majority of cases, remains children. This cultural-normative definition of women's role and the structural sex-based segregation merge to maintain women's status as confined to the family.

When women are expected to pursue their goals within the framework of the family, achievement outside of the home does not necessarily contribute to the elevation of their status. Their contributions to socioeconomic developments have not eased the burdens thay have at home.

Japan has embraced changes which, theoretically, should promote advances towards equality of women and men. The traditional, rigid sex-role ideology, however, has operated to confine women to much less than equal roles in contemporary Japanese society.

REFERENCES

Aoi, K. "Seimondai Saiko" [A reconsideration on sex issues], in *Gendai Nihon no Kazoku* [The Modern Japanese Family], edited by Kazoku Mondai Kenkyukai. Baihukan, 117–138, 1974.

Blood, R.O. and Wolfe, D.M. *Husbands and Wives: The Dynamics of Married Living.* The Free Press, 1960.

Dore, R.P., ed. *Aspects of Social Change in Modern Japan.* Princeton University Press, 1967.

Fujii, H., et al. *Nihon no Joshi Kyoiku* [Education of women in Japan]. Domesu Shuppan, 1973.

Goode, W.J. *World Revolution and Family Patterns.* The Free Press, 1963.

———. 1969. "Family Patterns and Human Rights," in *Marriage and the Family,* edited by Hadden and Bergatta, pp. 605–614. Peacock Publishers.

Institute of Population Problems, 1969. *Selected Status Concerning Woman Workers in Japan.* Research Series No. 193. Ministry of Health and Welfare.

Kaji, E. "The Invisible Proletariat: Working Women in Japan," in White Paper on Sexism—Task Force (ed.), Japanese Women Speak Out. WPSTF, 26–39, 1975.

Kobavashi, T. Fujin Rodo no Kenkyu [A study of women in industry]. Jichosh a, 1976.

Koyama, T. Gendai Kazoku no Yakurari Kozo [Role structure of the modern family]. Baifukan, 1967.

————. 1970. "A Rural-Urban Comparison of Kinship Relations in Japan," in Families in East and West: Socialization Process and Kinship Ties, edited by Hill & Konig, pp. 318–337. Mouton.

Kuroda, T. Nihonjin no Jumyo [The longevity of the Japanese]. Nihon Keizai Shimbunsha, 1978.

Kuroda, T. and Tachi, M. Jinko Mondai no Chishiki [The knowledge of population problems]. Nihon Keizai Shimbunsha, 1976.

Lebra, J., et al. Women in Changing Japan. Westview Press, 1976.

Masuda, K. "Gendai Toshikazoku niokeru Fufu oyobi Shutome no Seiryoku Kozo" [Conjugal and mother-in-law power structure of the modern urban family]. Konan Kaigaku Bungaku Ronshu [Konan University periodicals] 27 (1965): 49–66.

————. 1970. "Kateiishiki Chosa no Kaisetsu [An interpretation of a family consciousness]." Kobe-shi Chosa 14:77–78.

Michel, Andree, ed. Family Issues of Employed Women in Europe and America. Leiden: E.J. Brill, 1971.

Ministry of Education, 1975. Kyoiku Hakusho [White Paper on Education].

Ministry of Labor, 1974. Koyo Kanri Chosa [Survey on employment management].

Meguro, Y. Onna Yakuwari—Sei Shihai no Bunseki [A feminist analysis of the relations between women and men], Tokyo: Kakiuchi Shuppan, 1980.

Morioka, K. "Tokyo-Kinko Danchi Kazoku no Seikatsu-shi to Shakai-sanka" [Life history and social participation of Tokyo suburban family]. *International Christian University Social Sciences Journal* 7:199–277, 1968.

———. 1972. *Kazoku Shakaigakui* [Sociology of the family]. Tokyo: Daigaku Shuppan.

———. 1973. *Kazoku Shukiron* [Family life cycle]. Baifukan.

———. 1977. "Kazoku no Hendo" [Family change], in *Kazoku* [The family], edited by K. Morioka. Yuhikaku.

Nakajima, Kuni. "Meiji Kokka to Bosei" [The Meiji state and motherhood]. An oral report presented at a group meeting on Women's Studies, Tokyo on July 18, 1978.

National Institute of Vocational Research, 1967. *Fujin no Shokugyo to Raifu Saikuru* [Women's occupations and life cycle].

Nippon Hoso Kyokai. "Fujin no Ishiki" [Women's opinions] in *Yoron Chosa* [The opinion survey], June 1975, pp. 44–45.

Nojiri, Yoriko. "The Pattern of Conjugal Role Responsibility in Japan," in *Cross-National Family Research: Report on Conceptual Development, Pilot Testing, Field and Administrative Issues*, edited by M.B. Sussman. Submitted to Institute of Child Health and Human Development, Washington, DC, 296–322, 1974a.

———. 1974b. "Family and Social Network in Modern Japan: A Study of an Urban Sample." Unpublished doctoral dissertation, Case Western Reserve University.

———. 1976. "Diagakusei no Joseiyakuwari-kan" [The female role perception among university students], *Jochi Diagaku Shakaigaku Ronshu* [Sophia University studies in sociology] No. 1, 33–47.

———. 1977. "Kazoku Nettowaaku, Kazoku Shuki, Shakai Hendo" [Family network, family life cycle, and social change] in *Gendai Kazoku no Raifu Saikuru* [Life cycle of the modern family], edited by K. Morioka. Baifukan, 126–147.

Okada, Masako, et al. *Senmonshoku no Joseitachi* [Women in professions]. Aki Shobo, 1975.

Prime Minister's Office. *Fujin ni kansuru Ishiki Chosa* [Survey on women], 1973.

————. 1978. *Fujin no Genjo to Shisaku* [Facts and policies on women], Gyosei.

Research Committee on Women, 1974. *Gendai Nihon Josei no Ishiki to Kodo* [Opinions and behaviors of modern Japanese women].

Rodman, Hyman. "Marital Power in France, Greece, Yugoslavia, and the United States: A Cross-National Discussion," *Journal of Marriage and the Family*, 29(1967): 320–324.

Sodei, T. and Naoi, M. "Chukonen Josei no Seikatsu to Rogo" [Middle-aged women's life and their future], Tokyo: Rojin Sogo Kenkyusho, 1978.

Toda, Teizo. *Kazoku Kosei* [Family Composition]. Shinsen-sha, 1970.

Vogel, Ezra. *Japan's New Middle Class*. University of California Press, 1963.

Wimberley, Howard, "Conjugal-Role Organization and Social Networks in Japan and England," *Journal of Marriage and the Family* 35(1973): 1, 125–130.

Women's Organizations Federation, 1975. *Fujin Rodo no Jitsujo* [Present status of working women]. Ministry of Labor, 1975, 1977. Uoka Kaihatsu Senta. "Shofunno Ishiki to Kodo" [Housewives' consciousness and behavior] *Yoron Chosa* [The opinion survey], July 1975, pp. 28–47.

CHAPTER FIVE

Educating for
Responsible Citizenship

JIRO NAGAI

Soon after the surrender which ended World War II, the de-militarization and democratization of Japan were promoted swiftly by the General Headquarters (GHQ) of the Allied Occupation Forces. The new Japanese Constitution was put into effect on May 3, 1947, under the leadership of the GHQ. It is pacifist in nature, as illustrated by the Preamble:

> We, the Japanese people, desire peace for all time. . . . We desire to occupy an honored place in international society striving for the preservation of peace, and the banishment of tyranny and slavery, oppression and intolerance for all time from earth.[1]

The Fundamental Law of Education and the School Education Law were also proclaimed by the government along the lines of the Constitution in these early postwar years.

American education greatly influenced postwar education in Japan. For example, a 6-3-3 school system similar to the U.S. pattern was introduced. Social studies became a school subject in 1947 through the enforcement regulations of the School Education Law. Prior to World War II, history, geography, and civics were separate subjects in the curriculum. An integrated social studies curriculum based on the American pattern was introduced in the hope that it would contribute to the democratization of Japan. However, the new system created confusion for a time, since both teachers and the general public did not understand the new ideas. Morevoer, the conservative and the progressive elements of the nation seemed to interpret democracy very differently. For example, there was much discussion about the content of citizenship education among liberal-

---

[1]The Preamble to the Constitution of Japan, 1947.

democrats, socialists, and communists, whose political parties all became legal under the new constitution. Nevertheless, European and American democratic principles have formed the core of citizenship education in postwar Japan. As a result, Japanese children and youth have come under the strong influence of this postwar democracy, and the social studies curriculum has been a primary means of instilling democratic values.

The Korean War gave Japan a great chance for economic recovery. Since the conclusion of the San Francisco Treaty in 1951 followed by the U.S.-Japan Security Treaty, the Japanese economy has advanced steadily, thanks to the endeavors of successive governments and the people. Supported by this economic development, an education explosion took place in Japan as it did in many developed countries. The number of students in upper secondary schools, colleges, and universities increased greatly in the 1960s. Today, more than 90 percent of graduates from lower secondary schools advance to upper secondary schools, and almost 40 percent of upper secondary graduates go to colleges and universities.

This quantitative expansion of education has resulted in a perceived decline in school quality. The problem of the highly competitive entrance examination is serious. Entrance examinations remain one of the country's most difficult educational and social problems, and are seen as one of the main causes of student suicide, gangsterism, and classroom vandalism.

Recent economic and social changes have increased friction with the traditional culture and values. For example, the traditional role of women is rapidly changing, especially in urban areas. Women, formerly expected to leave their employment to raise their children after marriage, have returned to work in increasing numbers after childbirth, thus increasing the demand for nurseries in urban areas. Also, many serious problems have been raised for moral education and discipline by various social contradictions such as environmental pollution, disparity of ideologies, and generation gaps between value systems. While low by the standards of many other industrial nations, crime and delinquency are on the rise in Japan.

The necessity for better understanding of Japanese geography, culture, and history has been stressed by Japanese politicians across the political spectrum. The teaching of Japanese history and geography has been strengthened significantly under the umbrella of the social studies through revisions of school curricula and courses of study by the Ministry of Education (Mombusho). These new approaches are emphasizing national consciousness, patriotism, and responsible citizenship, combined with a revival of traditional conservatism. Since 1958, Moral Education (Dotoku), has been separated from social studies. It is an independent part of school curriculum and is compulsory in elementary and lower secondary education.

In the latter part of the 1960s, much social disorder was produced by the anti-Vietnam War movement and campus struggles of students in many Japanese universities. At the beginning of the 1970s, the Japanese economy was disturbed by the oil crisis. Fortunately, Japan was able to deal with these problems with minimal difficulty through the great efforts of the government and the people. At the present time, the Japanese economy is stable and prosperous. The international field for Japanese industry is being steadily developed, especially related to expanded trade networks. However, the Japanese people's value system is not settled, floating between progressivism and conservatism. Some undesirable tendencies to anti- or non-social attitudes are beginning to appear, such as a growing concern with self as compared to the group, the company, and the nation.

Japanese education has a responsibility for helping prepare youth for dealing with fundamental problems facing the nation. These include concerns about democracy, traditional culture, school entrance examinations, generation gap, environmental quality, energy, wise of natural resources, international perspectives, peace, and national defense.

Social and Educational Problems in Contemporary Japan

Except for some distinctive cultural elements, Japan and the United States of America display important similarities. Democratic political systems, a high degree of technological advancement, and highly developed industrial economies characterize both. Moreover, the two countries appear to have some of the same social and educational problems.

Contemporary Japan can be characterized as a "mass-society," with mass-production, mass-communication, and mass-education. Lifelong education is claimed. Yet, the role of higher education has changed drastically, and a certificate or diploma from a college or university cannot always secure better jobs, income, and social success. Even so, the entrance examination is becoming even more competitive in this highly school-oriented society.

Internationalization or globalization of people's lives may produce serious conflicts with their traditional culture and values. Consequently, today the Japanese are asking themselves, "What is Japan?" and "What should Japan be?"

Generational and ideological gaps relating to moral consciousness and the qualities of citizenship are becoming more marked in this complicated society. While the Japanese economy has prospered, cases of crime, delinquency, and what many call gangsterism among students in secondary schools have increased steadily. The moral consciousness of society is being lost day by day, and discipline training is declining in home and at school.

The Japanese are once again facing a major problem: "What should Japanese education be?" Japanese citizenship education is now expected to respond to these difficult questions. What, then, is present school education in Japan doing to develop citizenship?

The Present State of Citizenship Education in Japanese Schools

The phrase "responsible citizenship" is undoubtedly subject to various interpretations. In Japan, being a good citizen means being a democratic and world-minded citizen with a relevant, deep national identity. Therefore, citizenship education should produce citizens who:

1. realize that the dignity of the individual and respect for human rights form the basis of a democratic social life;
2. have a deep love and awareness of their own nation and culture and have a willingness to contribute to their advancement;
3. have a spirit of international understanding and cooperation, and a willingness to make contributions to world peace and the welfare of humankind.[2]

Schools in Japan are expected to develop such qualities in the nation's younger generation.

In contrast to American education, the Japanese system is centralized under the Ministry of Education. The consequences of centralization are obvious. For example, the course of study promulgated by the Ministry has a strong influence over school programs throughout Japan. The basic principles for curricula in elementary and secondary schools are prescribed by the Ministry through the Enforcement Regulation of the School Education Law. The standards of curriculum organization, the objectives, and the content of each subject are established and made public as "courses of study" for each school level. Each school is required to organize a suitable

---

[2]Jiro Nagai, "Social Studies in Japan," *Teaching Social Studies in Other Nations*, Bulletin 60 (Washington, DC: National Council for the Social Studies, 1979), p. 52.

curriculum for its specific conditions in accordance with the governing regulations and courses of study. The curriculum is then subject to the approval of the local board of education. Every textbook used in elementary and secondary schools must follow the course of study and must be approved by the Ministry.

Education for responsible citizenship is carried out within the structure of the entire curriculum, in the various academic subjects, in Moral Education, and in special activities at both elementary and lower secondary levels. The special activities at the elementary and lower secondary levels consist of the children's activities (e.g., pupil assembly, homeroom, and club activities), regular school events (e.g., ceremonies, cultural events, athletic meetings, school excursions, and safety guidance activities), and classroom guidance (e.g., school meals, health and safety guidance, guidance in the use of the school library, and other educational activities centering around the classroom).

Every school subject is related to citizenship education, but social studies plays an especially important role in this field. In the present course of study, the general objective of elementary social studies is stated as follows:

> To guide the children to deepen their basic grasp of social life, to nurture understanding of and affection to our land and history, and *to cultivate the foundation of citizenship necessary as members of a democratic and peaceful nation and society.*[3] (emphasis supplied)

Under this general objective, first graders learn about their immediate social environments—home, school, and neighborhood. Second graders learn about people who are engaged in various jobs in their daily life. Third and fourth graders learn about the community life in their own local districts. Fifth graders study the geography of Japan and characteristics of modern Japanese industry. Those at the sixth-grade level study the history of Japan, its cultural assets, and the function of Japanese government. Principles of good citizenship are emphasized throughout the elementary school social studies curriculum. As one can see, this curriculum closely parallels that used in many American elementary schools.

The general objective of lower secondary social studies is described in the course of study as follows:

> To have the pupils deepen their understanding of the land and history of their country from a broad perspective, acquire the basic education necessary as citizens, *cultivate the foundations of the qual-*

[3]Educational and Cultural Exchange Division, Science and International Affairs Bureau, Ministry of Education, Science and Culture, *Course of Study for Lower Elementary Schools in Japan*, Ministry of Education, 1978, pp. 31–57 (Social Studies).

ities essential to the members of a democratic and peaceful nation and society.[4] (emphasis supplied)

Social studies in lower secondary schools consists of three fields: geography, history, and civics. Geography and history are ordinarily learned concurrently in the seventh and eighth grades. Civics is taught in the ninth grade, which is the final year of compulsory education in Japan.

In geography, the time devoted to Japanese geography and world geography is approximately equal, and the latter is usually presented initially in the seventh grade, the first year of lower secondary school. In history, the ratio of time spent on Japanese history to time spent on world history is about 80:20. The field of civics includes social, economic, and political content. Here, the pupils study family life, social life, economics, politics, and international affairs, with an emphasis on the Japanese constitution.

The general objective of upper secondary social studies is stated in the 1978 course of study, to be enforced from 1982 on, as follows:

> To have the students deepen their understanding and cognizance of the society and humankind from a broad perspective, and *cultivate the qualities essential to the able members of a democratic and peaceful nation and society.*[5] (emphasis supplied)

Tenth graders are required to take a course entitled "Contemporary Society." This is a comprehensive social studies course integrating ethics, politics, and economics. Eleventh and twelfth graders take other subjects, such as Japanese history, world history, geography, ethics, and politics/economics, each of which is a separate elective.

The essential aims of social studies education from elementary through upper secondary school are to enhance children's awareness of society and to help them develop as citizens in a democratic society. Social studies is the primary curricular element for the promotion of responsible citizenship. Social studies promotes both cognitive and affective dimensions. The primary objective of social studies is to provide pupils with an understanding of society, and to support their desirable attitudes by establishing a firm foundation for correct moral decisions. This is reinforced through the Moral education curriculum, which is also very concerned with citizenship education.

---

[4]Educational and Cultural Exchange Division, Science and International Affairs Bureau, Ministry of Education, Science and Culture, *Course of Study for Lower Secondary Schools in Japan*, Ministry of Education, 1978, pp. 20–57 (Social Studies).

[5]Educational and Cultural Exchange Division, Science and International Affairs Bureau, Ministry of Education, Science and Culture, *Course of Study for Upper Secondary Schools in Japan*, Ministry of Education, 1978, pp. 53–61, (Social Studies).

Moral Education

Moral education in contemporary Japanese schools has deep roots in Japanese history. Traditionally, discipline and moral education were often equated and began in the home. Strict moral codes of behavior were taught in schools during the late 19th and early 20th Centuries. This strict code was replaced after the war with a new structure designed to be more flexible in nature than the dogmatic morality of the prewar period. Moral education as a subject area was to be taught along with social studies.

Moral education as a field of the school curriculum aims to internalize and deepen a sense of morality in accordance with the children's individuality and immediate environment. The present course of study for moral education, presented during one period per week in elementary and lower secondary schools, is based on four basic objectives:

1. To help the students comprehend basic behavior in daily life.
2. To enhance moral sense and cultivate ability to judge between good and evil.
3. To develop students' personality and establish their attitude towards creative life.
4. To foster eagerness and attitude as a member of a democratic nation and society.[6]

In association with other curriculum experiences, the aim of moral education is supplementing, deepening, and integrating the moral virtues acquired in the other educational activities and subjects. The objective is for pupils to develop an understanding of humanity, to enhance students' ability to make moral judgments, and to enrich their moral sense. The content of moral education relates directly to the development of responsible citizenship. For example, moral education in the elementary school is intended to help students:

> To understand the rules and significance of making rules by oneself, and to follow them willingly. It is desirable that, in the lower grades, one should learn to obey rules and regulations and, in the middle grades, to understand fully the significance of rules and regulations and obey them willingly, and to make good rules and make improvement in them if necessary.[7]

However, some people criticize this kind of moral education as not being moral in the true sense, but rather only an idealistic "list of virtues" approach. This objection is one of the reasons why teachers think this is a difficult field to teach and children dislike it. Con-

---

[6]Masatsuga Mase, "Moral Education in Japan," Paper given at IVth World Congress of the World Council of Comparative Education Societies. (Razan, Japan: July 7–10, 1980), p. 8.
[7]*Course of Study for Elementary Schools in Japan*, op. cit., pp. 200–205 (moral education).

sequently, the teaching of moral education is often more dependent upon the homeroom teacher's eagerness and efforts than the set curricular syllabus from the Ministry of Education. Moral education is, however, understood to be closely related to citizenship education.

In order to ensure some unity within the moral education curriculum, the Ministry of Education has published reference materials and guidance texts for teachers. A recent survey reveals actual practice in classrooms.

> In elementary schools, mainly supplementary readers on the market are used instead of the teaching references for moral education distributed by the Ministry of Education. Also, recently moral education programs on TV have been used frequently. . . . In junior high school, the teaching materials distributed by the Ministry of Education are being used now, but . . . usage of a supplementary reader is rising in popularity.[8]

Special activities during the school day are also an area in which moral education and disciplinary training are practiced. In almost every elementary school, a morning assembly of pupils and teachers is held before the day's first lesson. In every elementary and secondary school, sweeping and cleaning of classrooms and the school ground is a daily duty of pupils. To obey the school regulations is considered to be an important duty of children, even though cases of their breaking rules and acting rowdily have increased recently in secondary schools. School festivals, athletic meetings, school excursions, the entrance ceremony, and the graduation ceremony are all occasions in which disciplinary training is given to children. These are all extensions of moral and citizenship education.

Relationships between teachers and students are very significant in citizenship and moral education. In Japan, the teaching profession is traditionally respected. This attitude stems from Confucianism which was introduced into Japan from China in the ancient times and became one of the important elements of Japanese morality in the Middle Ages. Although the teachers' union insists that teachers are workers, many people, especially among the older generation still insist that teaching is a noble profession. Therefore, teachers are generally respected by parents and children. Furthermore, Japanese society expects that every teacher will be a good model for his or her students in citizenship and morals. In this

---

[8]Masatsuga Mase, op. cit., p. 9.

sense, Japanese teachers can be particularly influential in the areas of citizenship and moral education—perhaps even more so than American teachers.

There are problems which must be faced associated with moral education. These have been outlined by Professor Churo Nobe:

1. Many teachers have much difficulty with guidance during the hours of moral education, and so weaken their enthusiasm. They feel difficulty, firstly, in grasping the actual moral guidance provided in each field, and, secondly, in giving pupils a systematic and orderly understanding of the moral values following the demand to integrate and deepen the moral guidance in other fields.

2. Regarding the moral education through the instruction of subjects, the difficulty of a definite formulation of its roles, objectives and methods together with the variety of teachers' opinions make the teachers' efforts in this field rather ineffective as a whole.

3. In the case of moral education in the field of special activities and school events the situation is the same. It is extremely difficult for teachers to have enough understanding of the moral function of this field, to maintain an organic relationship with other fields and to provide a successful guidance in moral education in general.[9]

On the other hand, communities and parents have more control over education in the U.S. than in Japan. In Japan, only a slight connection can be noted between school education and out-of-school education, and Japanese parents do not have a strong voice in the matter of school operation, even in their PTA groups.

In the United States, religious and other special interest groups outside of schools play an important role in moral education. They can influence some elements of school education through parents and children. No religious group can be so influential over school education in Japan, although Buddhism and Shintoism are main elements of Japanese morality.

In any society, the closer the links among school, out-of-school, and home education, the better the citizenship and moral education will be. Because of the multi-ethnic character of its society, the United States may well have more difficulty than the homogeneous society of Japan in attaining a balance and coordination among the three kinds of education.

---

[9]Churo Nobe, "Fundamental Problems for the Improvement of Moral Education in Japan," Paper given at IVth World Congress of the World Council of Comparative Education Societies. (Razan, Japan: July 7–10, 1980), pp. 43–44.

A New Concept of Responsible Citizenship: Development and Prospects of Education for International Understanding

The contemporary world is shrinking rapidly. This situation is one result of the development of modern scientific technology and transportation, multi-national industries, and trade. Many contemporary problems in political, economic, social and cultural spheres occur in international relations. The welfare and development of one nation cannot be attained within its own territory or in some narrow region. They are related to the problems shared by all mankind. Interdependence among nations increases day by day. Moreover, the idea of world peace requires international cooperation.

These developments call for mutual understanding and cooperation among nations of the world. International awareness, world-mindedness, and a global perspective have become very important elements of responsible citizenship in contemporary society. In this sense, education for international understanding and cooperation must be given increased emphasis in the citizenship education in every nation.

Japan has been criticized for immature attitudes concerning international cooperation. This immaturity is largely due to geographical location and a historical absence of strong contact with other nations and cultures. Today's Japanese society has become internationalized very rapidly and the Japanese have also become more active abroad. Therefore, the Japanese people must improve their international attitudes. They must develop mutual understanding with other peoples, building up world-mindedness and an active desire to improve relations with others. Accordingly, the duty of schools in Japan is to promote education for international understanding and cooperation.

Since 1960, many Japanese people have been working abroad as a result of the development of the Japanese economy and industry. Many Japanese schools have been established in other countries for the workers' children. Thousands of these students return to Japan every year. The education of Japanese children who are abroad and also of those who have recently returned to Japan from abroad is becoming a serious new problem in Japanese education. This problem must be approached from the viewpoint of education for international understanding.

Japanese education has placed increasing importance on education for international understanding. One example is Japan's participation, since 1953, in the UNESCO Associated Schools Project in Education for International Understanding and Cooperation. Japanese Associated Schools have been actively engaged in this emphasis for over a quarter of a century. At the present time, four elementary schools, eleven lower secondary schools, and eight upper secondary schools are affiliated with the Project. The experiences and findings of the Project have contributed to revisions in the curriculum and study courses throughout Japan. This is viewed by many Japanese educators as a beginning of education for international understanding.

At the nongovernmental level, many organizations are active in international friendship and exchange programs. Among them, over 200 UNESCO Associations are especially visible and have significant programs. Under the influence of the UNESCO Associations, another two hundred UNESCO clubs have been developed in the nation's upper secondary schools.

In 1974, the Central Council for Education, one of the most important advisory committees to the Minister of Education, presented a report to the minister entitled, "On International Exchange of Education, Science, and Culture." It stressed the importance of developing education for international understanding and of improving international exchange activities in education, science, and culture in order to educate the Japanese people to be more active in, and make a greater contribution toward, international society. Since then, the council has promoted the spirit of international understanding and cooperation and has developed attitudes contributing to world peace and human welfare through programs for students. International education is one of the basic ideas implemented in the recent revision of the school curricula for all levels of Japanese education to promote citizenship education.

Summary

Japan has always had a strong tradition of citizenship and moral education. Discipline has been a cornerstone of both. Recently, the Japanese have begun to expand their concept of citizenship beyond the national level to the international level. The concept of citizenship education for international understanding is becoming more readily accepted. But much work still remains to be done.

REFERENCES

Anderson, Ronald S., *Education in Japan—A Century of Modern Development*, U.S. Department of Health, Education, and Welfare, Office of Education, 1975.

Educational and Cultural Exchange Division, Science and International Affairs Bureau, Ministry of Education, Science and Culture, *Course of Study For Elementary Schools in Japan*, Ministry of Education, 1978.

Educational and Cultural Exchange Division, Science and International Affairs Bureau, Ministry of Education, Science and Culture, *Course of Study for Lower Secondary Schools in Japan*, Ministry of Education, 1978.

Educational and Cultural Exchange Division, Science and International Affairs Bureau, Ministry of Education, Science and Culture, *Course of Study for Upper Secondary Schools in Japan*, Ministry of Education, 1978.

Mase, Masatsuga, "Moral Education in Japan," Paper given at the IVth World Congress of Comparative Education Societies. Razan, Japan; 1980.

Massialas, Byron G., *New Challenges in the Social Studies—Implications of Research for Teaching*, Wadsworth Publishing Company, Inc., 1965, pp. 200–203.

Ministry of Education, Science and Culture, *Educational Standards in Japan*, Printing Bureau, Ministry of Finance, 1977.

Nagai, Jiro, "Recent Developments of Education for International Understanding," *Bulletin of the Faculty of Education, Hiroshima University*, Part 1, No. 25, Hiroshima University, 1976.

Nagai, Jiro, "Social Studies in Japan," *Teaching Social Studies in Other Nations*, Bulletin 60, National Council for the Social Studies, 1979.

Nagai, Jiro, "The Theory of Education for International Understanding," *Bulletin of the Faculty of Education, Hiroshima University*, Part 1, No. 24, Hiroshima University, 1975.

Nobe, Churo, "Fundamental Problems for the Improvement of Moral Education in Japan," Paper given at IVth World Congress of Comparative Education Societies. Razan, Japan; 1980.

Omori, Teruo, "Japan: Tradition and Change," *Learning to Live In Society—Toward a World View of the Social Studies* (ed. Richard E. Gross & David Dufty), Social Science Education Consortium, Inc., Boulder, Colorado, 1980.

外国人の日本展望

Part II
Japan from an Outsider's Perspective

Assembling color television sets in Japan.

Photo courtesy of Japan External Trade Organization (JETRO).

CHAPTER SIX

Japan on the World Scene: Reflections on Uniqueness and Commonality

JACKSON H. BAILEY

Toward an Understanding of Japan

How are we to understand the Japanese and their culture? Are they the "Yankees of the East," as one 19th-Century observer commented? Are they "inscrutable Asians," as others imply? What forces are at work in Japanese life which, if identified, will give us insight into the true nature of this people and their accomplishments in the last half of the 20th Century? Clearly, we need this insight if we are to make sense of the world of the 1980s and beyond. We need it to make informed judgments about the political and economic policy alternatives which face the United States. We need it if we are to deal effectively with Japanese as individuals and Japan as a nation.

The current vogue in business circles in the United States which focuses on productivity, quality control, and personnel management suggests the need for much deeper and broader understanding of the forces which shape the lives of Japanese today. Alarmists call for import quotas on Japanese autos, as their counterparts a decade ago called for quotas on textiles and then steel. Yet, American agriculture and a host of other segments of the economic life of this country are deeply dependent on trade with Japan. Not just prosperity, but survival may well depend on deeper and better understanding of these forces. No longer is this merely "a good thing" in the abstract, advocated by altruistic internationalists. We must recognize the need in more basic terms.

There are several aspects of Japanese life and culture which are particularly important for us to examine as we seek the kind of insight which leads to understanding of Japanese character and motivation. One is the nature and role of religion and ethical values. A second is the nature of social structure and social relations. A third encompasses the role and effects of geography and relative physical isolation. A fourth is the nature of the modern experience of the Japanese itself. A century of struggle first to survive and then to "catch up" with the West produced social forces, institutions and ways of thinking which, on the whole, have served the Japanese very well. However, Japanese life has been so geared to this survival/catch-up process that Japan is now, in some ways, ill-prepared to play a new role in the world. Japan must not only learn how to play a role as world leader in the 1980s but the Japanese must learn to think and talk about themselves as the affluent people they have become. Japan is an economic giant yet the Japanese continue to think and talk as if theirs is a weak and poor country. This attitude is resented by people in other countries.

When we examine Japan and the Japanese it is very easy to fall into one of two traps. We tend either to talk about the uniqueness of Japanese culture and note how different the Japanese are from everyone else, or to look for the common heritage of all human beings and gloss over the peculiarities. These approaches need not be mutually exclusive, but if we are not careful, one mindset or the other may prevail. Clearly, reality lies somewhere in the "muddy middle." There are special characteristics and a distinctive flavor to Japanese culture, and these must be recognized if we are to understand the Japanese and communicate effectively with them. However, we must resist the temptation to take the next step, which all too often ends in the assumption that the Japanese language, aspects of its culture, and the people themselves are mysterious, unfathomable—in the end—"inscrutable." They are not. Below or beyond culture and distinctive cultural manifestations is a substratum of common humanity which links us all. We should resist attempts by the Japanese themselves (often subconscious attempts) and by the "experts" on Japan to lead or to push us in that direction. We can understand the Japanese, and they, us; but we must work hard to do so. We must develop and refine our questions, reject simple and simplistic analyses or explanations, and test our conclusions in open and honest dialogue with concerned Japanese.

Certain of these aspects of Japanese life and culture which we must examine are the products of the particular historical experience of the Japanese. Some have their roots in prehistoric time. Others are directly traceable to the recent past (specifically, the

Edo Period, from 1603–1868). In some cases, however, rather than being the result of factors from the historical past, these elements are a reflection of the contemporary scene and the forces that impinge on Japanese life right now. Perhaps the most significant example of this is the difficulty the Japanese are having in coming to terms with the fact of affluence in their lives. They still talk and act as if Japan were a poor, isolated country. Because of this they are reluctant to open their economic doors and to treat others as they have become accustomed to (and dependent upon) being treated elsewhere. Protectionist sentiment is as strong in their society as it is in ours. This is a serious barrier to international understanding, and they and we must address this issue openly and honestly if we are to survive and prosper in our interdependent world. I shall return to this issue later.

Religion and Ethical Norms

Are the Japanese "religious?" Pollsters and social scientists and "religionists" ask the question and carefully count numbers of people affiliated with religious institutions in Japan. The answers confuse and mislead them, and then they mislead us. Professor Byron Earhart in his brief introductory volume, *Japanese Religion: Unity in Diversity*,[1] and Professor Nakamura Hajime in his seminal study, *Ways of Thinking of Eastern Peoples*,[2] point us in the right direction. The thoughtful observer who lives in Japan confirms the truth of Earhart's and Nakamura's analyses. Indeed, the Japanese are "religious," if by that we mean that they seek to satisfy the universal human need for personal and societal meaning in existence, for norms of attitude and behavior which will allow people to live in harmony, and for a sense of continuity that goes beyond the lifespan of one person to the past and to the future.

The Japanese, individually and collectively, seek to commit themselves to values which transcend material existence and mere thirst for wealth and power. Their society, like ours, is engulfed by the enervating and pervasive effects of affluence, but thoughtful Japanese resist these trends and aspire to individual and national roles which will bear witness to those values.

Perhaps the primary and deepest value of Japanese culture is the recognition of what one scholar has called "the Ah-ness" of life. By

---

[1]H. Byron Earhart, *Japanese Religion: Unity and Diversity*, 3rd ed. (Belmont, CA.: Wadsworth Publishing Co., 1982).

[2]Hajime Nakamura, *Ways of Thinking of Eastern Peoples: India-China-Tibet-Japan* (Honolulu: East-West Center Press, 1964).

this, he meant a direct emotive response to the phenomena of existence—physical and spiritual. This response acknowledges the power and beauty that are present in the world. While not ignoring the forces of evil and the devastation that also exist, this perception focuses on the good, the beautiful, and the benevolent. In nature, the towering tree, the roaring waterfall, the quiet beauty of the dawn, clouds, and the sunset inspire it. In human affairs, the tender love of man and woman and mother and child, the bravery and courage of the warrior, and the dedication of someone to a transcendent cause awaken it. Each of these phenomena and a host of others are recognized as worthy of devotion, not primarily through intellectual and philosophical conviction, but more directly, in ways suggested by the sudden gasp of breath which, in contemporary American terms, means, "Wow! That's really something!" This value incorporates an aesthetic as well as a religious impulse. The aesthetic impulse is one of the well-springs of Japanese culture. In origin, we would call it Shinto (the indigenous native religious expression of the Japanese); in medieval times, it was taken up and developed by Zen Buddhism and then diffused throughout the culture until it has largely lost its direct religious force and expression. Yet it remains a vital element in Japanese life.

The institutional role of Shinto in Japanese history and culture is also profound. Shinto shrines dot the landscape throughout Japan and many are faithfully tended and continue to be a vital force in people's everyday life. From prehistoric times these local religious institutions have played a fundamental role, symbolizing and reinforcing people's sense of community. Buddhism did not challenge this role, for the most part, though there were exceptions, but rather played a complementary role. Over time there was a blending of the two traditions, sometimes formally through institutional and intellectual syncretism, often informally through a melding of practices and attitudes. Buddhism tended to emphasize the philosophical aspects of religious life and ministered to personal religious need while Shinto institutions nurtured communal values and linked the individual with the natural environment and the round of seasons. Beyond this, in modern times there was, of course, the manipulation of Shinto by the state as part of the ultranationalist-militarist phase of Japan's history.

Perhaps as old as these religious elements and certainly still powerful in Japanese life is a belief that human beings can relate best and most effectively in society in carefully defined hierarchical roles, which help to preserve harmony in a tightly organized and very crowded environment. Contemporary Japan is an effectively functioning democracy, with all the strengths and weaknesses that beset such a political order. The continued commitment to the value of status hierarchy in personal and individual fulfillment seems paradoxical. Yet, Japanese in their daily personal lives as well as in group behavior provide impressive evidence that both of these norms are operative. Status continues to be one of the major determinants of role; yet, there is impressive mobility in Japanese society, and Japanese appear committed to preserving both. The daily round of social intercourse for most people reflects the vitality of the commitment to hierarchy and the observation of social niceties as means to larger ends.

A third value which appeared early in Japanese cultural life and continues to characterize contemporary Japanese life is an introspective concern with the "inner landscapes of the mind." The Japanese invented the psychological novel, with the 11th Century masterpiece of world literature, *The Tale of Genji*. Modern authors have continued to probe the human psyche, seeking meaning and satisfaction in life through this exercise. Reinforced by the physical isolation of the Japanese islands, this value is often expressed in an unhealthy anxiety about what others—especially foreigners—will think. Excessive introspection may lead people to worry too much about what is going on in other people's minds. This concern with exploring and expressing inner thoughts and emotions has, I think, led to a formulation of human relations which gives primacy to "sincerity" (the Japanese term is *makoto*) as the touchstone and measure of the quality of these relations. "Makoto" as a value bewilders and frustrates the interpreter and the foreigner.[3] It is difficult to define, because it refers to motivation, as well as deeds and overt expressions of attitude. Employees in a labor dispute will accuse managers of lacking "makoto." They seem to be saying that the manager has not tried hard enough, but this is not primarily a complaint about results. To have "makoto" is to seek the truth in its deepest and fullest meaning and to witness to it in word and deed. This is a profound and potentially unnerving demand. It is small wonder that "makoto" defies simple explanation.

A fourth value which is seldom directly articulated, but often observed in Japanese life, is the emphasis on the "here and now." Japanese culture is activist rather than speculative. Japanese take the world and daily life as they come. They act, rather than muse about life. Even Zen meditation tends to prepare people to live in the workaday world, rather than removing them to another world. It is quite common now for Zen temples to organize and run weekend "retreats" for business men and white-collar employees. The

---

[3]Makoto is defined as sincerity, truth, faithfulness, honesty, constancy.

overnight program will include *zazen* (meditation), physical activity, menial labor or chores, and discussion sessions. The purpose is to help people live and work more effectively. In feudal times, this value was expressed in part by the role of the warrior in society, and, as that role declined in the 18th century, the norms were formulated in what is known as *Bushido* (the Way of the Warrior).

The term *Bushido* was established in the 18th Century by scholars and political leaders who saw the decline of the feudal values of a martial spirit, self-discipline and loyalty to one's lord. They attempted to codify these values and present them as the social and ethical ideal for the warrior class. "Weak in words but strong in action" said one commentator and modern Japanese have often witnessed that value.

Warrior values were preserved and transmitted into modern Japan after 1868 by two forces. One was Neo-Confucianism which was defined and implemented by the Meiji leaders in the period 1868–1890. It provided an ethical framework for Japanese life which emphasized loyalty and devoted service to the state. The other was the role of leadership which ex-samurai played in so much of Japanese public life—especially in business and in the armed forces—but in education as well. It is especially interesting to Westerners to note the impressive number and influence of people of samurai background who became Christian in the late 19th and early 20th Centuries. These people in leadership positions all displayed this same concern with the "here and now."

Another evidence of the focus on the "here and now" is the phenomenal growth of new religious groups which promise health and/ or wealth in this life rather than an after-life. These groups continue to grow as a social and religious phenomenon, though some, such as the Soka Gakkai, have come under public criticism for their authoritarian attitudes or through revelations of corruption.

A fifth value which pervades Japanese life—and seems to contradict the preceding one—is a sense of the place of individual lives in a continuum of existence reaching back into the dim past and ahead into the future. Japanese continue to be concerned about family and "name." Individuals make personal decisions for their own lives (basic decisions about marriage and employment, for example), giving important weight to their responsibilities to uphold, extend, and contribute to their family's name. Japanese friends once talked with us about whether their second son should take his mother's maiden name, perpetuating it after she and her sister died (there were no sons in their generation). This concern for the past and for the future is usually expressed in terms of human relationship and human experience.

Although this list is by no means exhaustive, the final value included here is the lack of exclusivity in value-orientation. Japanese culture has from prehistoric times been syncretic, gathering to itself and selecting for use those ideas, practices and institutions which seemed most relevant. Japanese have not felt that one should observe one set of practices and reject all those of alien cultures. Although Japanese writers and some leaders have occasionally advocated this, as in the 1930s, these cases have been exceptions.

The power of this outlook is illustrated by the foreign cultural elements that have gained wide acceptance among the Japanese, as well as those that have not. Christian missionaries and thoughtful Japanese speculate as to why institutional Christianity has not gained more strength in the culture. The great contemporary writer Endo Shusaku explores this theme time and time again. One reason surely is the strident demand of many of the missionaries (and their converts) for exclusive commitment to Christian creed and denial of the validity of all other traditions.* While the Japanese have been eclectic and adaptive, they have shown little concern for the niceties of consistency or the demands of exclusivity which are inherent in Western culture. The eclectic and adaptive forces in Japanese culture have, historically, been very powerful. We see this force at work even in Japan's pre- and early history with the incorporation of continental culture from Korea and China including Buddhism, Confucianism and the Chinese state system. The Japanese borrowed, and transformed radically, various of these cultural elements. One of the most fascinating of these transformations was the development of a phonetic syllabary from Chinese ideographs. (The Koreans also created a syllabary to use in writing their language.) This ingenious and effective invention made it possible for Japanese to write their own language and to develop a great literature in the 9th to 11th Centuries.

This aspect of Japanese culture reflects the geography as well as the historical experience of Japan. Set off physically from the Asian mainland and the rest of the world, the Japanese have periodically come into contact with other cultures and have learned to reach out eagerly to learn and to borrow. They are not, however, simply a race of borrowers. Their adaptive genius is evident everywhere in Japan. It is particularly striking in art and religion, but it is equally apparent today in business management and politics. The fact that they are not preoccupied with exclusive categories or inhibited about

---

*Another reason for this is the "closed-society" mentality which lays stress almost completely on the "in-group." A person is committed to and nurtures his relationship within the group thoughtfully and sensitively but almost any kind of behavior, even the violent and cruel, is acceptable when perpetrated on someone outside his own group. One can see evidence of this historically in the terrible persecutions of Christians in Japan in the early 17th Century and in the horror of the "rape of Nanking" in China in 1937 when Japanese troops raped, looted, and killed innocent civilians.

borrowing bits and pieces of things and ideas has equipped them remarkably well to deal with the complexities and demands of post-industrial life.

Here we have a set of values which are infused and reflected in ordinary people's lives. Some are expressed more clearly and directly than others. Some people exhibit some of them and not others, but I believe that, taken together, they go far toward helping us to understand the Japanese individually and collectively. "Ahness"—a direct emotive response to life—continues to be a palpable force in the lives of individual Japanese. They continue to assume that structure and hierarchy are positive values in social relations. They are concerned—often, overly concerned—with "what others will think," and they value deeply that subtle quality of "makoto" in human relations. Contemporary Japanese life is frenetically focused on the "here and now," not to the exclusion of larger perspectives, but with an emotional commitment and verve which is inspiring and at the same time a bit awesome. Japanese borrow freely and adapt elements from other cultures with little regard for continuity and consistency. In the process they transform these cultural elements and make them their own, creating new forms of cultural expression. Finally, Japanese as a people place much greater emphasis on the continuum of human existence from generation to generation than is usual in American society. Keeping these values in mind will give us clues to understanding Japanese behavior.

Social Structure and Social Relations

Superficial analysis of Japanese society and the Japanese leads easily to the conclusion that they are "groupy" and lack individuality (as evidenced by the widespread use of school uniforms, for instance). Such analysis confirms the analyst's sense of cultural superiority and thus does a double disservice. It results in our understanding the Japanese even less well than we did before, and we continue to wear our own cultural blinders.

A Japanese friend of mine, in the course of a discussion with American students who were talking earnestly about the importance of individual growth and independence, suddenly said to them, "But aren't you lonely?" He was shocked and concerned to see how they dismissed completely the value of family and group ties and the help and support which these can provide for the individual. They were taken aback by his comment. A fascinating discussion ensued as each side began to consider seriously the implications inherent in too much dependence or too much independence which our respective societies, at their worst, foster.

What does it mean to be a person in Japan? This question is so fundamental that we often fail to ask it, assuming that we know. "After all, they are human beings like us, aren't they?" It is not an easy question to answer. Clearly, however, the answer will not be the same for a Japanese as for an American, because the historical and contemporary life experience of people in Japan is so different. Historically, especially over the last three centuries, the Japanese experience has been one of intense crowding in a fundamentally urban environment. The center of gravity of Japanese life culture, particularly the leading edge of change and development, shifted from the rural countryside to such urban centers as Edo, Sakai, and the castle towns which had developed by the 17th Century. The warriors, dominant in setting social values, came to live in cities, and over time they were imbued with urban values. Contrast that with the American "frontier spirit" which, until the recent past, has informed our vision of what it is to be most fully human.

In Japan, individuals live, move, and have their being within an environment which forces them to accept the discipline of the group in order to survive with any sense of satisfaction and self-fulfillment. We see evidence of this in family life, in education, in business and the professions. This does not mean that there is no place for the individual or individualism in Japanese life but its expression takes different forms.

The most obvious opportunity for individual expression in Japan is in the arts in all their forms. Here people can give free rein to imagination and expression and wide diversity is acceptable. At the same time, paradoxically, that freedom is usually expressed by transcending and transforming established form and technique, not by rejecting or flouting them. Actors, artists, and artisans all see artistic expression as grounded in intense and extended training, practice and discipline in technique. Once skills and techniques have become second nature one can transcend them and enjoy true freedom and individuality.

Many Japanese would see social structure and even hierarchy as fostering rather than restricting social interaction. They provide patterns which enable social intercourse to take place without forcing people constantly to choose how to carry on such relationships. At their worst, these norms are restrictive, preventing new people and new ideas from emerging and contributing to national life; at their best, they free people to maximize their contribution to society. Japanese themselves vigorously debate these issues, which arise frequently in discussions of contemporary problems in trade, diplomacy, politics, and education.

It is easy to overemphasize the role of hierarchy in Japanese social relations. This tendency has been reinforced by the translation of the writing of Professor Nakane Chie—particularly, her book, *Tate no Shakai* (Vertical Society).[4] Less well known is the work of anthropologist Professor Yoneyama Toshinao, who emphasizes the egalitarian role of the "nakama" (support group), which in informal ways effectively counters the restrictive, authoritarian nature of formal hierarchical structures.[5]

Infusing Japanese social relations is the high value placed on "indirection" as an operative principle. Most Westerners have heard of the role of the "go-between" who mediates many facets of life from marriage to politics to business deals. Japanese abhor social confrontation and will go to great lengths to avoid it. In a crowded urban environment and a culture which puts a premium on grace, refinement, and civility in everyday life, this aversion is powerfully reinforced by both positive feedback and negative sanctions. American students who go to study in Japan are nonplussed by these patterns and often are upset by them. "Why didn't she tell me?" is the cry when they discover that their Japanese mother was upset by some word or action. It can be clumsy and annoying to have to go through an intermediary but it can also save a lot of wear and tear on the psyche to have a third party mediate the relationship.

If we are to understand Japanese social structure and social relations, we shall have to observe carefully how Japanese interact in large groups and in twos and threes, and not seize too quickly upon a simple generalization that Japanese like to be in groups.

Geographical Isolation

Shima-guni—island country. How often one hears this phrase when Japanese speak or write of their country. This physical fact has had profound influence on Japanese life and cultural attitudes. Until the military defeat of World War II, the Japanese had always been able to control access to the islands from the outside. They have, at times, reached out to other cultures avidly to grasp and adapt ideas and material goods to their own uses. At other times, they have closed themselves off, virtually isolating themselves from contact with the outside world.

This isolation and control over outside contacts has led to the development of the Japanese sense of being a special people. The relative ethnic homogeneity of the Japanese reinforces this attitude.

---

[4]Chie Nakane, *Tate no Shakai* (Vertical Society); published in the U.S. as *Japanese Society* (Berkeley: University of California Press, 1972).

[5]"Basic Notions in Japanese Social Relations," in Jackson H. Bailey, ed., *Listening to Japan* (New York: Praeger, 1973).

When our first child was born in a Japanese hospital in 1951, we suddenly confronted the startling reality of this homogeneity when we viewed the 30 cribs with infants in the hospital nursery. In one was a pinkish bald baby; all the rest held "look-alikes" with lots of black hair. There was no doubt who was the foreign baby! In the 1930s, the flames of militarism and ultra-nationalism were fed by this idea of Japan as a special place and the Japanese as a special people with a mission for the world. The concept in one form or another persists. It is most frequently expressed in two ways.

First, it persists in the notion that the Japanese and their language are so special and peculiar that the foreigner cannot really grasp or fully understand either. Japanese will regularly say about someone who has studied the language, "For a foreigner, he speaks and understands Japanese well."

A second and even more disturbing piece of evidence of the "special people" theme is the persistence of racism in Japanese life and thought. Japanese are prone to deny this and, when pressed, like to point the finger of criticism at other people and their racial problems. However, the fact remains that Japanese society is fundamentally racist and closed to the outsider. While there are exceptions, and thoughtful and sensitive Japanese are working for change, basic societal attitudes in these matters are deeply ingrained. We find that when there are Blacks among the college students whom we send to Japan to study (and we have them frequently), we must take great care in selecting families for them to live with and in interpreting the presence of a black student to the family, if we are to avoid unpleasant treatment of the student. Further, Japanese treatment of minority groups within the society (Koreans and the so-called "burakumin,"* especially) provides graphic evidence of racist attitudes, even though, strictly speaking, these minorities are not racially different from mainstream Japanese.

The persistence of this "island country" mentality is perhaps the greatest challenge the Japanese face in the world today. The need for access to resources and markets occupies most of the time and energy of national leaders. Yet, as the demand by the rest of the industrial world for access to the Japanese market grows, the Japanese face a grave threat if they do not address the need to change these basic attitudes toward the outsider. Until the mid 19th Century they could afford the luxury of an exclusionist policy. Since

---

*The term "burakumin" is a shortened euphemism for "tokushu burakumin," or special hamlet people. Traditionally, these people have worked in slaughtering, leather work and other jobs associated with "pollution" of a social or physical nature. Western literature often referred to them by the term "eta," which is the cultural equivalent of "nigger." There are about 2,000,000 "burakumin." Some live in ghetto segregation, and many suffer discrimination in marriage and employment. As a group, they have been restricted in occupation and as to where they can live.

then they have done a magnificent job of reaching out, absorbing culture and material goods from the outside world, and of "catching up" with the West. They have not, however, confronted the challenge of the "island country" mentality in an interdependent world which resents the way in which the Japanese treat foreigners unless they are in some way "guests" or fall into special categories.

At the same time, we must recognize the great strength and cohesiveness which this experience of isolation and control of contact with the outside world has brought the Japanese. By turning inward as they did in the Edo Period (1603–1868) and refining and developing internal institutions and modes of thinking and acting, they distilled a cultural tone and wove a tough social fabric which have in the 20th Century been creative, productive, and resilient to a remarkable degree. High productivity and quality control in the 1980s are not the result of the persistence of feudal values. Still, the sense of social cohesion and the willingness of the Japanese to work hard, in what have been perceived as a series of great national efforts for survival, bespeak a cultural heritage of great strength and adaptability.

From Survival to Affluence

"We are a poor country struggling to survive." For a century, from 1868 to 1970, this analysis of Japan's position in the modern world was essentially accurate. In the fifteen years following Commodore Perry's first visit to Japan with the "Black Ships," Japan was rent internally by political struggle and violence and besieged from without by the demands and threats of the Western powers. Out of these fires was forged a psychology which served the Japanese well for a century, but which threatens now to bring all their gains to naught. The "survival/catch-up" mentality which emerged was a pragmatic response to the realities of the world of the 19th Century—a world dominated by Western imperialism and an emerging "social Darwinist" mentality which the Japanese took seriously and some took literally.

Japan in 1870 *was* a poor country with few material resources. The country was vulnerable to attack from without and political unrest within. The leaders of the Meiji Restoration—young, able samurai, already tested and experienced as administrators in their own domains—quickly established priorities and objectives which would speak to the realities of the world as they saw it. They coined the slogan, "Enrich the country, strengthen the military." These dicta became the guiding principles for a frenzied national effort which persisted with remarkable continuity and momentum for 75 years.

The cost in human terms was staggering; yet, the benefits, in certain ways, were enormous, too.[6] Education and most aspects of social and political life were made the handmaidens of the state and were often corrupted or distorted by this pressure. The environment was, in many cases, despoiled in the name of national survival, and Japan left a trail of torture, death, and destruction in its colonies—especially Korea—which lives in the memories of other Asians to prejudice relationships even today. Yet, in the brief span of seven decades, Japan and the Japanese burst on the world scene demanding recognition. They bring with them a rich heritage of art, culture, and social experience which have in substantial, if subtle, ways already changed the way we live and perceive our world. Such words as tycoon, honcho, and skosh, borrowed from Japanese, as well as the work of Frank Lloyd Wright and Ernest Fenollosa, attest to this.

Today, in the 1980s, the effects of Japan's presence in the world community are even more evident, and again, as in the 1930s, we hear cries that the Japanese pose a threat to our well-being. The quality of Toyota cars and Nikon cameras now set the standards to which others aspire even while they protest the Japanese threat.

The dynamics of this psychological process of interaction between our two societies are fascinating to observe on both sides of the Pacific. There is much that we need to learn about each other if we are to weather the current storm. We need to listen to their concerns, but equally they need to hear and attend to ours.

The story of Japan's development from a poor isolated feudal society to a modern post-industrial mass-producing and mass-consuming world power has too often been termed a "miracle." It is a remarkable story, but not a miraculous one. Others have chronicled it well. The best introductory works are John W. Hall's *Japan from Prehistory to Modern Times*, for institutional development, and Edwin O. Reischauer's *Japan, the Story of a Nation*, for narrative history, and *The Japanese*, for contemporary analysis.[7] Beyond the story itself, we should note in particular two elements in Japanese culture and historical experience which are often overlooked.

The first is the adaptive genius which the Japanese have displayed time after time as they have encountered new ideas and new ways. It was evident in prehistoric times in their acquisition of horses and swords, and in the 7th to the 9th Centuries in their assimilation of Chinese culture. In the 16th and 19th Centuries, the

---

[6]See Mikiso Hane, *Peasants, Rebels and Outcastes: The Underside of Modern Japan* (New York: Pantheon Books, 1982), for an account of some of the human cost.

[7]John W. Hall, *Japan: From Prehistory to Modern Times* (New York: Dell, 1968); Edwin O. Reischauer, *Japan: The Story of a Nation*, 3rd ed. (New York: Knopf, 1970); and *The Japanese* (Cambridge, Mass.: Harvard Univ. Press, 1977).

Japanese turned their attention to Western culture. Superficial analyses usually dismiss this as "mere copying." "The Japanese are a nation of borrowers," say some with scorn. Yet, at one level, aren't we all? American culture is, to a large degree, an amalgam of elements "borrowed" from English and continental models. It was not until well into the 20th Century that we could shake off that sense of being beholden to other peoples and cultures for our own identity. The Japanese have proceeded at forced draft for more than a century in a frenzied attempt to catch up with the West, and one of the prime elements in that effort has been the borrowing and adaptation of material and spiritual elements of Western culture all the way from steam engines to political and economic structures. This has left little time for the digestive process which is required for native genius to come through with distinctive new inventions.

One astute observer, Professor Hidetoshi Kato of Gakushuin University in Tokyo, suggests that the inventive/creative genius of the Japanese lies in "chemical" transformation, rather than in the invention of new things or ideas. He uses the metaphor of the chemical process which produces *tofu*, the soft soy bean curd which is a staple in the Japanese diet, likening Japanese culture to the brine which transforms the soy beans into curd (a new product), rather than the curd itself.[8] He suggests that the Japanese of the 21st Century may well contribute to the world culture through this adaptive genius, rather than through new inventions as such. In some sense we already see this happening with such adaptations of method as quality control circles which originated in the work of Edward Deming, an American, but which have been adapted and transformed by Japanese management to become a pivotal force in Japanese industrial life and are now being brought into American industrial life.

The second element which is often not recognized is the long experience that the Japanese have had in coping with crowded urban living. Edo, the political capital of Tokugawa Japan (1603–1868), was probably the largest city in the world in 1800. The norms of Japanese social and cultural life were developed and established by townspeople and merchants in the 18th and 19th centuries. This happened only very slowly in the West after the industrial revolution. In Japan it occurred before the industrial revolution and modernization. There, townspeople established the normative role of urban life in what was structurally still a feudal society. As the process of urbanization gained momentum in Japan in the 20th Cen-

---

[8]"Soy Bean Curd and Brine" in Bailey, *Listening to Japan*, pp. 3–6.

tury, it built on a foundation already more than 200 years old, and it was infused with cultural and artistic values which, at their best, display a creative vigor unparalleled in few other places and times. (This is not to ignore or deny the poverty, degradation, and misery which are the reality for many people in an urban society, but to underline that in the case of Japan, as perhaps in Vienna of the early 19th Century, urban culture has been an especially powerful and creative force.) It is no accident that Tokyo in the 1960s and 1970s had no less than six major symphony orchestras and a host of other cultural institutions patronized not only by an elite upper class, but by ordinary people from all walks of life. Urban living and urban values in Japan are more than a response to capitalist industrialization and modernization.

Let us return to the issues of survival and affluence. We have seen the strength and effectiveness of the theme of survival as a motivating force in Japanese life in the last century. In the 35 years since the end of World War II, the power of this force has diminished little. In fact, survival continues to be the leitmotif of Japanese life at most levels—even in the midst of peace, prosperity, and affluence. Herein lies the problem. The Japanese struggled with every nerve and fiber through the 1950s and 1960s to survive and then to catch up. Having shucked off the bonds of militarism and ultra-nationalism which had held them on the narrow road to disaster in the 1930s and 1940s, they were free to focus their attention and apply their energies to building a new society and a prosperous economy. To a remarkable degree, they were successful. Democratic patterns, rooted in prewar experience and nurtured by the American Occupation and the institutional grafts which in many cases "took," became part of the fabric of Japanese political and economic life. Even the return to public life of purged conservative and right-wing leaders such as Kishi Nobusuke, who had been a member of the Tojo Cabinet, did not alter the basic thrust of this process.

New stresses and old problems appeared in the late 1960s as the single-minded devotion of national energies to economic development produced environmental degradation of monumental proportions. A generation of young people, products of postwar prosperity, struck out in often blind and violent protest against the inhumanity of "examination hell" at home and of Japan's collaboration with the United States as a staging area for the Vietnam War abroad.

Yet, by the mid 1970s, Japan had weathered these storms, as well as the Nixon shocks (restrictive surcharges on imports and the opening of diplomatic relations with the Communist government in Peking) and the first oil crisis. While Japan's economy was in the doldrums, the environment was being cleaned up and strict new environmental control laws were put in place, triggered by landmark court cases won by citizen groups through democratic processes. Symbolic of these changes was the fact that Mt. Fuji, which could be seen from Tokyo only three or four times a year in the late 1960s, could, by the late 1970s, be seen 40 to 50 times.

By 1980, two issues had emerged as the major agenda items for the nation. The first of these, defense and rearmament, had smoldered for three decades as an endemic problem for Japan and for United States-Japan relations. Occasionally, the smoldering had heated into flames, as in the 1960 demonstrations which produced the May and June riots and finally resulted in the cancellation of the Eisenhower visit and the resignation of Prime Minister Kishi. Japan's postwar constitution forbade the maintenance of land, sea, or air forces (Article Nine). At the behest of General MacArthur and the American Occupation authorities, the Japanese had established military forces beginning in 1949 under the euphemistic name "National Police Reserve." By 1954, this name had been transformed into "Self-Defense Forces," and the process of providing a legal justification was under way. Since then, these activities have been justified legally by reference to Japan's "inherent right of self-defense." There has been steady pressure from the United States to increase Japan's commitment to defense build-up and rearmament. A majority of the Japanese have come to support the current level of spending and the present status of the Self-Defense Forces, but there remains very strong resistance to expansion of the forces or basic change in their nature by equipping them with offensive as well as defensive weapons. There was a major political storm in the Diet in the spring of 1982 when it was discovered that the SDF had budgeted funds to retrofit F-15 fighter planes with bomb racks for air-to-ground missiles. Heavy public and private pressure on Japan from the Reagan Administration for a more rapid defense build-up and for participation in military missions outside Japan's territorial waters by naval and air units have been resented and resisted in Japan.

The other issue on the agenda is trade and balance of payments. Japan has profited tremendously from the free-trade system which evolved in the world after 1945. The Japanese have been clear in their support of the system in world-wide terms, but as a country Japan has been slow to open its markets to outsiders. Even though formal tariff barriers have been gradually reduced and are now, with a few exceptions, lower than in most other countries, two factors have combined to make the Japanese market very difficult to enter. The first has come to be known as "non-tariff barriers." Requirements of inspection, licensing, and customs clearance have been excessive and cumbersome. Foreigners see them as evidence of collusion between government and business to restrict entry into the Japanese market, and they are frustrated and angry over the bureaucratic red tape in which they find themselves entangled.

The second factor has, so far, received little attention. It results from the nature of the Japanese domestic distribution system. In structure, the system has many layers, and relationships among producer, distributor, and retailer make it very difficult for most foreign firms to break into the Japanese market directly and independently. This situation gives foreigners a sense that they are being frozen out of a potentially lucrative market while Japanese firms can easily go directly into U.S. and European markets. The Japanese protest that the foreign firms make little effort to learn the Japanese language or to tailor their marketing strategies to the peculiarities of Japanese consumer needs and tastes. The facts suggest that there is substantial truth in both positions.

In the controversy surrounding these two issues, defense and trade, we have the evidence of a dramatic and fundamental shift in Japan's position and role in the world. This change has created a context in which the very attitudes, values, and strategies which have served the Japanese so well and have propelled Japan to the center of the world stage now become a source of misunderstanding and resentment and a potentially serious liability.

For more than a century Japan was "resource-poor" and had to play catch-up with the advanced industrialized world. It has developed a "we try harder" psychology which has been remarkably successful. Now it is not weak; it is not poor by any material measure (though it still has few raw material resources of its own); it is not even isolated any more. The problem is that the Japanese are finding it very difficult to accept these realities and reorder their policies and relationships to make them consistent with these facts. They still talk as if they were poor, weak, and isolated, and this is irritating even to their friends. Perhaps their most formidable task in the 1980s is to learn how to think and talk about themselves, their country, and their aspirations in new terms. If they do not do so, they will be in for some very troubling times. We have seen how effective and successful the Japanese can be at catching up. Now, they must develop their talents as regional and global leaders. This is the real test that confronts them.

Important as it is, even this change in perception will not be sufficient to smooth the path of Japan's relations with the rest of the world. Japan is still a closed society and in some sense a racist society, as well. Here again what has been a strength can become a serious weakness. The cohesive sense of social unity which has given Japan and the Japanese the toughness of fiber and the spirit to pull themselves up by their bootstraps twice in a century is ugly and counterproductive when it turns aside with condescension or contempt the foreigner's attempt to understand and get inside the culture. Japanese welcome the foreigner as visitor and guest. They welcome the beginner's attempts to learn language and to understand and admire cultural excellence. However, when foreigners cross the threshold and attempt to meet the Japanese on their own cultural terms in their own language, they are frequently rebuffed. Most Japanese have not even recognized the need to change, to say nothing of trying to do it. As they begin to come to terms with Japan's new role and status, they may then be able to address this even more difficult question of how to open up a society that has been closed for so long.

Conclusion

As we look at Japan and the Japanese and attempt to understand them and our relationship to them, it seems clear that we must redouble our efforts to understand in their terms—not just in ours. What does it mean to be Japanese in the 1980s? Whether we examine religious experience and ethical norms, social structure and social relations, or the realities and pressures of the historical events of the last century that have shaped the Japanese world view, we become aware of significant differences between them and us. Yet, underneath those differences we share a common humanity.

Americans and Japanese find themselves in a most improbable "love affair." Even in the 19th Century there were evidences of this. Since World War II, the relationship has blossomed and been remarkably fruitful. It is not without its problems and hazards.

The Japanese can be fully as enthnocentric as we, and the more intertwined our relations and our national interests become, the more dangerous are these inherent problems. The arrogant demand of the United States for more defense spending on the part of Japan and for direct participation in joint military activities outside Japan is matched by the self-righteous indignation of the Japanese in pretending that theirs is an open society and that foreigners have free access to their markets.

Japanese "style" in social relations differs radically from Americans' sense of the importance of free and easy interaction. This leads to frustration and misunderstanding on both sides. Obviously, each side needs to work hard if we are to minimize friction and tension. Yet, remarkably, Americans and Japanese continue to "hit it off" well in a host of formal and informal contacts. We should celebrate that reality and continue to work together to enhance the overall relationship which is so vital to our respective roles in the world of the late 20th Century.

日本に関する授業活動及び教材

Part III
Activities and Resources for
Teaching About Japan

This is the Ginza—Tokyo's downtown.

Photo courtesy of Japan External Trade Organization (JETRO).

CHAPTER SEVEN

Teaching About Japan in Elementary and Secondary Social Studies

DONALD O. SCHNEIDER

Currently, inclusion of Japan in the social studies curriculum presents an interesting contrast. Japan is a frequent subject in elementary programs, but receives inconsistent treatment at the secondary level. Since the 1950s, Japan has often been included in elementary textbooks and courses as a subject for cross-cultural study of institutions and customs. At the secondary level, Japan has been regularly included in world geography and world and United States history courses. Japan is also frequently selected for inclusion as a case study in a variety of other courses for dealing with selected phenomena or issues, such as population pressures, natural resources distribution and utilization, technological development, environmental problems, and cultural adaptation and change. However, the treatment of Japan in secondary textbooks is usually limited in scope and perspective, sometimes incorporating errors, and, in the case of Japanese-U.S. relations, is sketchy and ethnocentric, especially in United States history texts.[1]

What should we teach about Japan? At the primary level, given children's developmental patterns and the current status of social studies instruction, in-depth study of Japan appears inadvisable. Elements of Japanese culture can be used, along with comparable examples from other cultures, to illustrate many of the topics, concepts, and ideas typically discussed in primary social studies programs. Seymour Fersh recommends that instruction at the elementary level focus on broadening children's perceptions of human experience, and on new ways of helping them understand and ap-

---

[1]The Japan-U.S. Textbook Study Project, *In Search of Mutual Understanding* (Bloomington: Indiana University, 1981).

preciate themselves and others.[2] Content dealing with Japan should
be used to challenge students' assumptions about the way things
are, or should be, eliciting reactions such as: "I never knew that
. . .," "I never thought of that . . .," or "I never felt that . . .."[3]
As children are led to such responses, they are sharpening their
cognitive skills of comparing, contrasting, inferring, etc. Language
provides a good example. Japanese is written vertically from right
to left instead of horizontally from left to right. Consequently, books
read in reverse order as compared to ours. The Japanese also structure their language differently. The placement of subject, verb, and
object differs from the standard English language pattern. "I like
baseball" would be ordered as "I baseball like" in Japanese syntax.
Students can learn by brief encounters with elements of Japanese
culture as well as other cultures that what seems "natural" and "right"
to us is not universally perceived in the same way. People have the
need to communicate, but may create and use a variety of languages and other means of communicating that can be effective and
esthetically pleasing. In recognizing this, students develop a broader
understanding and greater appreciation for humanness and cultural
variety.

As students move into the upper middle and lower secondary
grades, Fersh suggests that we increasingly emphasize the process
by which a culture functions—that is, why and how a culture developed the way it did.[4] Instead of focusing upon a single topic as
in the early elementary grades (with Japan providing one of several
illustrations), the instructional content could now include several
topics or elements of a single culture in order to teach students to
see the interrelationships of these elements and to develop a better
understanding of and feeling for the culture. At this middle level,
students can be given opportunities to consider Japan's geographic
setting—its proximity to China, yet the importance of its physical
isolation in relation to its particular historical development and its
creative cultural adaptation of ideas and institutions borrowed from
others.

For older students, at the upper secondary level and beyond,
Fersh suggests expanding the knowledge base. Elective courses are
to be rich in a variety of content about the history, geography, and
culture of a society. But another approach might also be considered—a return to using Japan as a case study in dealing with se-

---

[2]Seymour Fersh, *Japan in the American Classroom* (New York: Consulate General of Japan,
Japan Information Service, 1977), pp. 8–9; Seymour Fersh, *Asia: Teaching About/Learning
From* (New York: Teachers College Press, 1978), pp. 10–14.
[3]Fersh, *Asia: Teaching About/Learning From*, p. 13.
[4]*Ibid*, p. 15.

lected topics and issues. Whether through interdisciplinary courses dealing with contemporary world affairs, global issues, or future studies, or in single disciplinary courses such as sociology or economics, elements of the Japanese culture and experience can provide a variety of illustrations for fruitful study.

The Asia Society's publication, *Opening Doors: Contemporary Japan*, provides a useful scheme for organizing either a separate study of Japan or a study of Japan as a part of a world studies program.[5] Units on contemporary life, perception, and expression, decision-making, identity, and values focus on basic human needs in the context of the Japanese experience and help students understand the ideas and processes of change, interdependence, conflict management, and coping with differences from another cultural perspective. The authors suggest how some themes and ideas could be used to organize a comparative study of other cultures.

Those who wish to stress a global perspective in teaching about Japan will find *Intercom* #84/85 especially useful in presenting a rationale, a delineation of necessary student competencies, and key concepts to be used as themes in organizing instruction.[6] The four competencies are: (1) perceiving how one is involved in the world system biologically, ecologically, socio-culturally, historically, and psychologically; (2) making decisions about one's lifestyle in adjusting to imposed and uncontrollable changes, identifying the transnational consequences of personal and group decisions, and taking into consideration the interests of others, including those of future generations; (3) making judgments which involve perceiving choices, collecting and processing data, and recognizing the value of others' experiences as guides to dealing with issues and considering models of alternative futures; and (4) exerting influence through lifestyle decisions, work-related activities, social action, and political activities. The authors discuss the importance of four major concepts or themes central to a global perspective: conflict, change, interdependence and communication. Content selection, always a challenging task, becomes more manageable and often more rational when concepts such as these are used as organizing themes.

What follows are some suggestions for teaching activities related to some of these concepts and competencies and some of the key ideas suggested by other writers of this Bulletin. These suggestions are representative and illustrative, rather than comprehensive. Some are more appropriate for elementary students; others, for more advanced students.

---

[5]*Opening Doors: Contemporary Japan* (New York: The Asia Society, 1979), pp. ix–xxiii.
[6]David C. King and others, *Intercom* #84/85, *Education for a World in Change: A Working Handbook for Global Perspectives* (New York: Global Perspectives in Education, 1977).

Initiatory Activities

IDENTIFYING STUDENT PERCEPTIONS OF JAPAN

Activity 1. Elementary/Secondary   It is often very useful to determine what images and attitudes students have about other peoples and nations before launching into a formal study of the society. Instruction can then be adapted to student needs, making the most efficient use of available time and resources. This strategy also permits assessment of student knowledge gains through pre-statements and post-test comparison. For elementary students, simple open-ended statements may be used:
 · When I think of Japan, I think of . . ..
 · When I think of Japanese people, I think of . . ..
If the instructional unit will include a comparative dimension, the statements may be adjusted to provide this focus:
 · Japan is . . ..
 · The Japanese people are . . ..
 · The U.S. [or other nation] is . . ..
 · Americans [or other national group] are . . ..
Students should answer these questions individually on a sheet of paper. With young students, two or three responses may be all that are desired. Older students may be asked to list as many things as they can think of. Responses may then be listed on the chalkboard or, preferably, an overhead transparency, or sheet of newsprint or butcher paper for later reference. Students' papers may be collected and saved for comparison with responses to the same questions at the completion of the unit. A follow-up discussion could identify common elements of perception, possible misperceptions or stereotypes, and specific characteristics associated with the Japanese, American, or other selected culture. Areas where more information is needed could be identified by questions such as:
 · Why do you think that?
 · How could we find out if that is really so?
 · Where do you think we might get the information we need to tell if that is true?

Activity 2. Elementary/Secondary   As a follow-up activity, present students with a series of photographs covering a range of subjects, such as topographic features, climate/weather, industries, transportation, leisure activities, rural/urban settings, and exteriors/interiors. The photos should depict the range of contrasts and variations found throughout Japan. For example, photos should depict the snow-covered mountains and flatlands of Hokkaido in winter, as well as the lush green mountains and terraced fields of southern Honshu or Kyushu in summer. The class may be organized into four or five small groups and each given several of the collected photos to compare with the listing of responses previously recorded from the pretest. The photos can be collected from books and magazines, many of which are available free from Japanese consulates. Two excellent sources are back issues of *Japan* and *Japan Pictorial*, which contain photographs of excellent quality on a wide range of subjects.

Alternatively, slides can be used for a whole-class activity. The collected photos can be made into slides or commercially available slides can be used.[7] A two-screen presentation can be used to show contrasts in landforms, climate, industries, traditional and popular culture, and other topics. The contrasting scenes could then be compared with students' pre-tests responses.

Activity 3. Elementary/Secondary In a variation of the above activities, students can be asked to identify things about Japan and the Japanese that fall into each of three categories: (1) those that are very different from the U.S. experience; (2) those that contain both similarities and differences; and (3) those that are very similar to the U.S. experience. The items for consideration could be food, housing, clothing, work, music, sports, transportation, communication, and others. Several photographs or slides illustrating the "typical," as well as those showing the range of Japanese experience, might then be presented for student analysis.

STUDENT PERCEPTIONS OF THE INTERDEPENDENCE OF JAPAN, THE UNITED STATES, AND OTHER NATIONS

Activity 4. Secondary For secondary students, study might begin with a consideration of how a series of hypothetical events might affect each of the following: themselves as individuals, the United States as a nation, and Japan. Some possible events are:
1. A war in the Middle East that results in a sharp reduction of world oil supplies.
2. A decision by the major industrial nations of the world to raise import duties on selected "non-essential" and luxury goods such as automobiles, cameras, musical equipment, and consumer electronic goods.

---

[7]For excellent commercial slide sets, write to: International Society for Educational Information, Inc., Michiko Kaya: Kikuei Building No. 7–8; Shintomi-2 chome, Chuo-ku Tokyo Japan. Especially recommended is the set entitled: *The Japan of Today II: Climate and Way of Life*. These may also be available for loan through Japanese consulates.

3. A widespread, prolonged summer drought in the midsection of the United States.

4. An announcement by an international panel of experts that high concentrations of poisons have been found in numerous species of salt water fish from virtually every corner of the globe.

5. A sharp increase in the exchange rate of the dollar against most of the world's major currencies.

6. A move by Third-World nations to set up a series of organizations similar to OPEC to regulate prices of various metals, minerals, and natural resources.

Activity 5. Secondary A related initiatory activity involves the preparation of a file of articles from newspapers and magazines on Japan. Prior to the commencement of the unit of study, the instructor should collect articles dealing with Japan or Japan-U.S. relations for a period of several weeks. As an opening activity, the teacher can have the students read and classify the articles according to a set of categories such as: trade/economy, politics/foreign relations, social/cultural life, resources/energy, and environment/ ecology. Capable students might generate their own categories. After classifying the articles, the students can analyze them more carefully.

· What impressions do we obtain about Japan from the articles?
· Can we learn any Japanese points of view about the selected topics from the articles?
· What do the news media think that Americans want to know, or what is important for Americans to know about Japan and Japan-U.S. relations?

These two activities will begin to suggest to students the many kinds of events that may affect people of both nations directly, although sometimes differently or with different degrees of intensity. They will also underscore the global significance of certain kinds of trends such as our increasing interdependence and need for international cooperation and cultural understanding in resolving many issues.

CREATING A BULLETIN BOARD OR LEARNING CENTER TO STIMULATE INTEREST

Activity 6. Elementary An interesting activity that can be used at the elementary level to initiate a study of Japan and used subsequently to guide class or individual study is one involving a "mystery" bulletin board or learning center display. The teacher sets up a display consisting of news headlines, photos, Haiku poetry, artifacts, books of stories or folktales, and magazines that depict various elements of Japan and the Japanese way of life. The various media can be grouped around questions or problems that encourage students to hypothesize about their identity, significance, and meaning. Initial speculations can be used as a basis for group projects, individual research tasks, or class activities guided by the teacher using pre-selected materials.

Activity 7. Elementary   One example of a follow-up activity is a matching exercise. Large travel posters depicting scenes in Nara, Kyoto, Tokyo and other Japanese cities are available from travel agents, Japan Airlines, or Japanese consulates. Typically, these have the name of the city below the photo itself. The names can be cut off and each poster numbered. Students can then be asked to guess the city, using visual clues (modern buildings, religious shrines, etc.) and subsequently researching each possible city, using atlases, travel brochures, textbooks, back copies of *Japan* or *Japan Pictorial*, and other materials, many of which are available from Japanese consulates. Much the same thing can be done using newspaper or magazine articles, poetry, and short stories, by detaching the headlines or titles from a photocopy of the original. The activity can be enjoyable, while providing purposeful reading. It can be used to initiate a general study of Japan or to focus upon a selected aspect of Japanese experience.

The Japanese Setting

GEOGRAPHICAL FACTORS: LOCATION

Activity 1. Upper Elementary/Secondary   Japan's location—its island isolation, on the one hand, and its closeness to China, on the other—the topographic features of its land, and its resource base all have had a profound effect in shaping Japanese history and culture. Some time should be devoted to helping students understand how geography has helped to shape the Japanese people's frames of reference about their own nation and the world. Elgin Heinz suggests an interesting activity for upper middle grades and secondary students to help them begin their study.[8] He suggests having students draw a map of the world on a sheet of paper from memory without any available sources. Tell students to approximate

---

[8]A. Elgin Heinz, "Utilization of Resources, Natural and Human," in *Opening Doors: Contemporary Japan*, pp. 123–24.

landforms, not worrying about accuracy of boundaries or coastlines; simple geometric shapes will suffice. The objective is to reproduce relative sizes, locations, and shapes. Heinz suggests that after students have had time to draw their maps, teachers draw a world map, labeling continents and selected countries as they proceed. Where most students will have America in the center of their maps, the teacher's map should show Japan in the center with Asia to the left and the Americas to the right. In a follow-up discussion, the teacher could ask:

- Why did you place the countries or continent you did in the middle?
- What difference would it make to perceptions of the world if Japan is in the center rather than Europe or the U.S.?

Activity 2. Secondary   The concept of ethnocentrism could be introduced and discussed in relation to one's world view. Both the students' and the teacher's maps could then be compared to a small-scale world map (wall map) or to maps in textbooks or other comparable sources. The teacher could ask students:

- Where is Japan located?
- Is it likely that maps in Japan would be like the students' maps and those in American textbooks or like the teacher's? Why?

Activity 3. Elementary/Secondary   Since maps are flat, they distort reality. Using a globe, students can locate Japan. Then they can view Japan from different perspectives—from China looking east, from the north pole looking south, etc. The teacher can have them consider:

- Does looking at the globe give you a different perception of Japan's location? In what way?
- Does mainland United States seem further away? Why do you think this is the case?
- Which states are closest to Japan? (Use a piece of string to measure).
- Which nations can be considered Japan's neighbors?
- When it's daytime here, what time of day is it in Japan? What time would it be in London? Moscow? New Delhi? Peking? Bangkok?

Activity 4. Elementary   Using a piece of string, have the students locate one end at Tokyo and extend the other to Anchorage, Alaska. Have them move the string in an arc. Ask them:

- What nations are included in the arc?
- Why can we say that the U.S. is one of Japan's neighbors?

Young children could be asked to locate Japan on a slate globe (this type usually does not have names of countries on it). Then other nearby countries could be named. Using a string and chalk they could be asked to draw an arc whose outer extent would reach mid Alaska. The discussion questions suggested above could then be adapted to their maturity level.

Activity 5. Elementary/Secondary It is not uncommon for Americans to think of Japan as located more toward the equator since they often think that Japan has a tropical climate. While using a globe, have students note its latitudinal location. Have them compare it with that of the United States and Europe. Have them speculate about the climate in each of the four main islands. To enhance their understanding, consult Reischauer's *The Japanese*, page 12, which shows Japan superimposed over the east coast of the United States.[9] The four main islands stretch from northern New York, New Hampshire, Vermont and Southern Maine to Southern Georgia and Alabama. Prepare an overlay transparency set drawn to the same scale using the United States map as the base and the map of Japan as the overlay. Use a third overlay to locate major cities of comparable latitude: For example, Sapporo/Manchester and Boston; Sendai/Washington, DC; Tokyo/Raleigh; Kyoto/Chattanooga; and Nagasaki/Atlanta. Alternatively, Japan might be superimposed over the west coast of the U.S.

With younger students, a globe rather than a flat map might be used. A transparency drawn to the globe's scale might be used to superimpose Japan over the east or west coast of the United States. In addition to helping students develop a locational perspective, this activity can be used to stimulate a study of comparative climates, topography, and demographic patterns.[10]

SIZE

Activity 6. Upper Middle Grades/Secondary As Yasuo Masai pointed out, Japan is considered to be a small country by the Japanese as well as Americans. In comparison to its giant neighbors, China (PRC), the USSR, and the U.S., it is small, but in a global context Japan is considerably larger than average. It ranks 55th in size among 161 nations. Students from the middle grades on can get this general idea by comparing Japan's land area to that of several nations around the world. Many students will be surprised to find that Japan is

[9]Edwin O. Reischauer, *The Japanese* (Cambridge, Mass.: Belknap Press, 1978).
[10]Adapted from John J. Cogan, in "Teaching About Japan in the Elementary School," *Georgia Social Science Journal*, 12 (Summer 1981), pp. 18–21.

larger than several European nations, including the United Kingdom, West Germany, and Italy. Provide students with a list of nations. Include some European, African, Southeast Asian, and Latin American nations of various sizes. The number will depend on whether students are to work independently or in groups. Using atlases, almanacs, and other available references, they should find the total land area of each nation in square miles or kilometers or both. Record the data on the chalkboard, overhead transparency, or large sheet of paper. Ask the students to rank the nations in order from largest to smallest. Help students analyze the data with questions such as:

· Where does Japan rank? Near the bottom? Near the middle?
· Looking over the world map or globe, are the nations on our list representative in size?
· What would be a reasonable generalization about Japan's land area?
· Given the fact that Japan is larger than average, how might we account for the fact that the Japanese perceive their nation as small?
· Why do we think of Japan as a small nation?

POPULATION

Activity 7. Elementary   Although Japan ranks in the upper middle range among nations in land area it currently ranks seventh in the world in population. Its population is about one-half that of the United States, which ranks fourth. (118 million compared to 229 million.) Its population density—approximately 810 people per square mile—is one of the highest in the world. The United States has a population density of 63 people per square mile. Japan has about one-half as many people on 1/25 as much land. John Cogan suggests an interesting activity to help elementary students comprehend this reality.[11] Teachers can divide the classroom, playground, or gymnasium into twenty-five spaces of equal size. (A string coated with colored chalk, held tauntly at the ends and snapped against the floor or paving, will mark the spaces quickly and easily.) The students are informed that these twenty-five spaces represent the land area of the United States. One space outlined in a different color chalk represents the entire land area of Japan. Students distribute themselves over the twenty-five spaces; then half of them try to squeeze into the specially marked space, quickly learning something about population pressure! (This activity should be used

---

[11]*Ibid.*

in conjunction with one that helps students visualize Japan's land area as larger than average; otherwise, students will erroneously assume that Japan is smaller than average.)

Discuss with students their perceptions and feelings about their experience in crowding:
- How did you feel?
- What sort of problems might this create?
- How might these problems be handled?
- Does this mean that all of Japan is crowded?
- Are some areas of the U.S. this crowded? Which ones? Are these areas subject to the same problems?

Activity 8. Upper Elementary Responses to some of the above questions might be recorded and used for subsequent comparison after further study. For example, students may list housing, transportation, pollution, unemployment, and crime as "problems." The latter two are not problems for the Japanese on the scale experienced in some other nations, whereas the first three are significant concerns with which the Japanese have had to contend.

Activity 9. Middle Grades/Secondary To extend students' understanding of relationships between people and land, introduce the idea of usable land. Have them consult maps, atlases, and other sources to answer the question: How much of Japan's land is usable? Only about one-sixth of the square set aside as Japan in the activity suggested earlier is suitable for agriculture or large concentrations of people. Most of the rest is mountainous terrain. Of the twenty-five squares set aside to represent the U.S., about ten are adaptable for agriculture and large-scale population concentration. Engage students in a brainstorming session:
- How might the Japanese try to use their available land to its maximum?
- How might farms and farming practices differ in Japan and the U.S.?
- Japan is an island nation. How might the sea be important to the Japanese people?

Using their speculations to guide their research, students should use available textbooks, atlases, almanacs, filmstrips, films, and other resources to test the validity of their responses. A particularly interesting source is *The State of the World Atlas*, which provides an outstanding array of maps and map charts.[12] The one on "The State by Population" is a graphic representation of nations by pop-

---

[12]Michael Kidron and Ronald Segal, *The State of the World Atlas* (New York: Simon and Schuster, 1981) $11.00—paperback.

Table 1. Population Figures for Selected Nations

Nation	Area (Millions of Sq. Miles)	Rank[1]	Population (Millions—1981 Estimate)	Rank[1]	Population Growth Rate %	% Urban	% Under 15 Years Old	% Literate	Life Expectancy M	Life Expectancy F
Japan	145	55	118	7	1.1	76	24	98	73	78
China (PRC)	3,690	3	985	1	1.5	25	32	55[2]	60	63
Germany (FR)	96	71	61	12	−0.1	92	20	99	68	75
Mexico	762	14	70	11	2.5	67	42	70	63	67
UK	94	73	56	14	0.0	76	22	99	68	74
USA	3,615	4	229	4	.8	74	22	99	69	75
USSR	8,650	1	268	3	0.9	65	26	98	64	74

[1]Rank among 161 nations
[2]Estimates range from 25% to 85%
Sources: Compiled and sometimes averaged from several sources, including the Population Reference Bureau, *1981 World Population Data Sheet;* UN *Statistical Yearbook,* 1978; *Information Please Almanac,* 1982.

ulation size rather than actual land area. (Other perspective maps, such as those on National Income, Trade Power, and Food Power could be used for topics discussed below.)

An Interdependent Japan in a Global Setting

Comparing and contrasting, stock-in-trade teaching techniques, are powerful tools. Although they are sometimes criticized because inappropriate use may result in reinforcing ethnocentric perceptions and negative stereotypes of others, comparing and contrasting almost invariably come into play when students attempt to integrate unfamiliar content with existing knowledge and perceptions. With careful guidance from the teacher to avoid undesirable we/they thinking, comparisons can add greatly to students' understanding of others and themselves as part of an interrelated system.

Some comparisons have already been suggested, such as those dealing with population density in the U.S. and Japan. Here are some others that may help to extend students understanding of Japan in a global context.

Activity 1. Upper Middle Grades/Secondary Reproduce Table 1 as a hand-out or transparency. Have students consider the questions below in groups or individually, and then have them discuss their answers. After class discussion, ask them to write one or two generalizations that the data suggest about Japan in relation to the other nations listed.

- How does Japan compare in land area to other nations? How does it compare to the European nations listed?
- How does Japan compare in population?
- Which nation is most densely populated? Which is least? (Use the figures from the area and population columns to compute the density per square mile.)
- Which nations are growing fastest? Which, if any, had a decline in population?
- Which nation is the most urbanized? Which the least? How does Japan rank?
- Which nation faces the biggest task of educating its people? (Consider population size, literacy, and especially population under 15.)
- What do the life expectancy data suggest about the Japanese and the quality of life in Japan in comparison to other nations?

Table 2.   Japanese Exports and Imports in Millions of U.S. $, 1970

Category	Exports	Imports
Foodstuffs	1,208	14,416
Raw Materials	1,331	22,850
Fuels and Crude Oil	369	45,354
Chemical Products	6,012	4,956
Machinery/Transportation Equipment (includes motor vehicles)	58,475	7,038
Motor Vehicles	21,601	737
Other Industrial Products	34,508	14,416
Total Manufactured	98,995	26,410

Source: Japan Institute for Social and Economic Affairs, *Japan, 1981, An International Comparison.*

Activity 2. Upper Middle Grades/Secondary   Table 2 provides a list of Japanese imports and exports. Reproduce the table as a transparency or hand-out, or create a pie graph from the data, and ask students to consider these questions:
- What does Japan import more of than it exports?
- What does Japan export more of than it imports?
- What does this tell us about Japan's economy? Is Japan self-sufficient?
- In what ways is it dependent on other nations?

Activity 3. Upper Middle Grades/Secondary   Tables 3 and 4 provide additional comparative data on some indicators of standard of living. Table 5 provides information about the prevalence of some consumer goods among the Japanese. The tables may be reproduced and given to students. They provide quantifiable data and

Table 3.   Some Standard of Living Indicators for Selected Industrialized
Nations

Nation	Per Capita Daily[1] Intake		Per Capita GNP in	Per Capita Annual[1] Consumption (kg)		Communications		
	Calories	Protein (Grams)	U.S. $ (1980)	Energy[2]	Crude Steel	Phones[3]	TV Sets	Newspapers[4]
Japan	2,949	87	8,902	4,260	512	424	239	526
Germany (F.R.)	3,381	85	13,383	6,627	538	374	311	312
Italy	3,428	98	6,908	3,438	368	285	220	113
UK	3,336	92	9,280	5,637	349	415	317	388
USA	3,576	106	11,536	12,350	618	744	571	287

[1]Data for latest year available, 1977–79
[2]Coal equivalent
[3]Per 1,000 population
[4]Circulation per 1,000 population
Sources: Data Services Limited, New Delhi, Statistical Outline of India, 1982; Japan Institute for Social and Economic Affairs, Japan 1981, An International Comparison; Information Please Almanac, 1982.

reflect a Western, industrialized, materalistic orientation to assessing standards of living. Students should be cautioned that these are not the only considerations. Judgments about the "quality of life" will depend on a number of factors, including whether the items listed in the tables are valued by people. Before using the tables, teachers might brainstorm with students about those things that enter into judgments about the quality of life. Love, status, a sense of personal worth, and feelings of well-being and security are some other factors, and these are not quantifiable.

Questions for Table 3:
·   What indicators of standard of living does this table include?
·   Are these adequate to measure standard of living? What other factors should be considered in assessing the quality of life in a particular country?
·   Using the indicators in the table, how does Japan fare in comparison? Japan uses less energy than Germany and the United Kingdom, yet produces more total goods and services (second only to the U.S.). How can it do this?
·   What might account for a lower caloric intake in the Japanese diet as compared to the other nations? Is their diet not as "good," or just different?
·   Look at the figures on communication. Compare newspaper circulation to TV sets in Japan and the U.S. What do these data suggest?

Questions for Tables 4 and 5:
·   Have prices gone up more sharply in the U.S. or Japan? In which category have prices gone up most in Japan? Can you

Table 4.   Japan and U.S. Consumer Prices and Wage Level Trends

	1979 Consumer Price Indexes (1967 = 100)						1978 Real Wage Index[1] (1967 = 100)		
1970 Total Indexes	Food	Clothing	Housing	Transportation	1979 Total/ Indexes	1970–1979 Increases	1970	1978	1970–1978 Increase
Japan 119.3	271.9	212.9	212.9	287.3	261.5	119%	137.2	208.7	52%
U.S. 116.3	234.5	166.6	227.6	212.0	217.4	86%	102.2	112.0	9%

[1]In Manufacturing Industries; takes into account inflation in prices, so equates how much dollars in 1978 could buy at 1967 prices.
Sources: United States Department of Labor, Bureau of Labor Statistics, *Handbook of Labor Statistics*, 1980; Japan Institute for Social and Economic Affairs, *Japan 1981, An International Comparison*.

Table 5.   Ownership of Selected Consumer Goods by Japanese Households, 1970–1980

	Ownership Rate %	
Item	1970	1980
Refrigerators	89.1	99.1
Washing Machines	91.4	98.8
Color TV	26.3	98.2
Vacuum Cleaners	68.3	95.8
Cameras	64.1	82.9
Passenger Cars	22.1	57.2
Stereos	31.2	57.1
Air Conditioners	5.9	39.2

Sources: Japan Institute for Social and Economic Affairs, *Japan 1981, An International Comparison*.

think of any reasons? (Japan is energy poor and must import proportionally more oil than the U.S.)
· The Real Wage Index takes into account cost of living increases. It tells how much more purchasing power wages earned in 1978 had over wages earned in 1970. Which nation's manufacturing workers had more real wage increases during the 1970s? What are some reasons for this? (More goods produced per dollar invested because of more efficient plant, equipment, or workers; bigger market for goods.)
· What does Table 5 tell about ownership of consumer goods in Japan?
· Which goods showed the strongest advances in ownership? Can you suggest reasons for this pattern?
· What does this table tell us about the level of wages and salaries among Japanese workers?
· How do these trends compare with those in the U.S.?

Table 6.   Average Japanese Household Budget, 1980

Item	% of Disposal Income
Food	22
Housing, Fuel & Lights	08
Clothing	06
Medical Care	02
Reading & Recreation	07
Savings	22
Other	33

Source: Japan Institute for Social and Economic Affairs, *Japan 1981, An International Comparison.*

Activity 4. Middle Grades/Secondary   Having students look at an average Japanese family's budget may provide some surprising comparisons to their own. Ask students to discuss with their parents approximately what percentage of the household income goes for food, clothing, housing, utilities, savings, and all other expenses (label this category "other"). Instruct them to bring in percentage estimates only, not dollar estimates. Individual averages can be used, or a class average can be derived. Have students compare their family budgets with the percentages provided in Table 6. What differences do they find? Are they surprised at the percentage saved in Japan? (In mid-1982, the savings rate in the U.S. averaged just over 6%.)

Activity 5. Secondary   In recent years economic and trade issues have arisen between Japan and other nations. Especially acute has been the issue of Japanese auto imports to the U.S. Create a bilateral "citizens meeting" dealing with auto trade. Ask students to play the roles of the following: A Japanese auto company executive, a U.S. auto company executive, a Japanese auto worker, a U.S. auto worker, a U.S. consumer, and a Japanese consumer. Have students research their parts to identify key issues, major positions taken by the Japanese and Americans, and possible ways of resolving the issue. For younger students or those with limited research skills, provide a fact sheet or listing of the key ideas on individual role cards. One group may be asked to role-play the situation while the rest of the class observes. The students can then be asked to discuss their perceptions of the activity. Alternatively, the class may be subdivided into groups so that all may participate in the role-playing. In preparation, develop a research file of data and articles about Japan. From this file, the more capable students could identify important facts for use in creating fact sheets or role cards. Other students may collect news articles and editorials and consult consumer product reports (e.g., see the annual April issue of *Consumer Reports* for automobile quality and maintenance ratings; see also the chapters by Yoshiro Kurisaka and Linda Wojtan for factual material or sources for additional data).

Understanding the Japanese: Values, Tradition and Change

What does it mean to be Japanese? In earlier chapters Mizone and Bailey identified three important elements: the Japanese concern with self-discipline, the importance of status in their relations with one another, and their selective preservation of tradition and adoption of cultural elements from others. These ways of behaving, of responding to one another, and of viewing the world are based upon values. Standards of worth, or values, are those things that influence every aspect of our lives. By recognizing them, we can come closer to understanding other people and perhaps ourselves. Here are a few suggested activities that will enable students to consider those values that make the Japanese the people they are and enable students to compare some Japanese values to their own.

USING FOLKTALES AND STORIES TO LEARN ABOUT JAPAN

Activity 1. Elementary Gerald McDermott's *The Stonecutter* is a beautifully illustrated publication that will appeal to younger students.[13] Brief and easily read to students, it is a retelling of a Japanese folktale about a stonecutter's foolish longing for power. The tale opens by describing the stonecutter, Tasaku, happy at his work chipping away at the mountain. "He asked for nothing more than to work each day . . . .." One day Tasaku observes a wealthy, powerful prince and his entourage in a magnificent procession. His personal contentment turns to envy, and his secret wish is answered by the spirit that lives in the mountain on which he practices his craft. He is transformed into a prince. But his initial joy soon turns into discontent as his princely experiences reveal his limited power. One day, while walking in his garden, he becomes envious of the power of the sun and asks the spirit in the mountain to turn him into the sun. Once again, his new power brings an initial burst of joy only to give away to discontent as he comes to realize that clouds can limit the effect of his energy. His envy again consumes him, and again the spirit answers his wish. The now familiar cycle re-

---

[13]New York: Puffin Books (Pengiun Books), 1978. First published by Viking Press, 1975.

peats itself. Initial joy in the exercise of power—as he blankets the earth with storms—gives way to discontent as clouds strike the mountain and their power dissipates. Tasaku demands to become a mountain. The spirit of the mountain complies, but in so doing leaves Tasaku, because there is nothing further it can do for the stonecutter, who is now mightier than all. The tale ends with Tasaku feeling "the sharp sting of a chisel . . . [of a] . . . lowly stonecutter, chipping away at his feet." "[D]eep inside, he trembled."

This tale has a familiar ring to it, with universal appeal and meaning. It can serve as an excellent springboard for a discussion of values. Even young children can consider questions such as the following:

- What is happening to Tasaku as the story ends? What can he do about it?
- Have you ever felt the way Tasaku did—that you wanted to be someone or something else?
- Have you ever dreamed of doing something or having something such as a particular toy and then eventually doing it or getting it? How did you feel at first? Did your feelings change? Were they similar to Tasaku's?
- What do you think Tasaku learned from his experience?
- What can we learn from this story?
- Since this is a story that older Japanese might tell younger Japanese, what does it tell us about what some Japanese think is important in life? Do you think many Americans would agree with this idea? Have you ever heard a story like this told in America?

Activity 2. Elementary Whereas *The Stonecutter* is a Japanese tale printed in English, J.B. Lippincott's publication of Mirjoka Matsutani's *How the Withered Tree Blossomed* includes both the Japanese text and English translation side by side.[14] It is designed to be read like a Japanese book—the cover opens with the spine of the book to the right, not left, as in our tradition. The book is also beautifully illustrated by Yasug Segawa.

This is a delightful story of a diligent, hard-working, honest old man and wife who are satisfied with but little in life and who make the most of what they have. They are continually deprived of what is theirs by a greedy, overbearing, lazy neighbor and his wife. The story begins with the theft of the kind old man's fish from his fish trap, in place of which the neighbor leaves an old root. The old man makes the best of it, drying and splitting it to make firewood.

---

[14]Mirjoka Matsutani, *How the Withered Tree Blossomed* (Philadelphia: J. B. Lippincott, 1969).

Instead, the root becomes a dog. The dog grows and leads the old man to buried treasure. The neighbor and his wife take the dog, but when it fails to lead them to treasure, they kill and bury it. From this soil grows a willow tree. The old man cuts off limbs from it to make a wooden bowl memento. The jealous neighbors take the bowl, only to have food turn to filth in it, and in disgust they burn it. The sad old man and his wife ask for the ashes, and when the angry neighbor throws them, they touch an old withered tree in the old man's yard. Immediately it blossoms. The jealous neighbor, trying to obtain an undeserved reward from a passing prince who is duly impressed by the flowering tree, prances around with the remaining ashes, claiming that he is able to make withered trees blossom. But ashes fly into the eye of the prince, who bans the neighbors from his realm, and the old man and his wife live happily ever after.

Questions similar to those posed about *The Stonecutter* can be asked of children. As they come to understand the basic elements of the story ask them:

- Can you tell what the Japanese author thinks is important in life from this story?
- Are there people like the old man and his neighbor in our society?
- Does the story have meaning for us?

Activity 3. Middle School/Secondary John Bester's translation of Kenji Myazawa's *Winds from Afar* (1972) provides a collection of sixteen tales that have meaning for adults as well as children.[15] Some are very short, such as "Dahlias and the Crane," and can easily be read to students. Others are longer, but rarely exceed ten or twelve pages. Myazawa's sensitivity to the world of nature is a striking feature of the stories. Widely popular in Japan, these stories also have universal appeal. They can be read simply for pleasure when individual students have finished assignments early, or they can be used as a basis for class activities or discussions similar to those suggested above.

TRADITIONAL AND CHANGING JAPANESE LIFE

Activity 1. Middle Grades/Secondary *Facts and Figures of Japan* (updated annual editions available free from Japanese consulates) provides some data that can be used to shed light on contemporary Japanese life.[16] On page 135 of the 1980 edition is a table showing

---

[15] Available from Kodansha International, Ltd., 599 College Avenue, Palo Alto, CA 94306.
[16] *Facts and Figures of Japan*, 1980 edition (Tokyo: Foreign Press Center).

Table 7.   How Japanese Adults Spend Their Weekdays[1]

	Sleeping	Eating	Working	Housework	Commuting	Watching TV	Other
Men	8:06	1:30	7:15	0:27	0:59	2:58	4:29
Women	7:36	1:37	3:46	5:18	0:28	4:02	4:41

[1]Totals are for more than 24 hours because some activities are engaged in simultaneously.
Source: Foreign Press Center, *Facts and Figures of Japan* (1980).

Table 8.   How Japanese and United States High School Students Spend Their Time (in %)[1]

	Studying		Watching TV		Helping in Home		Away from Home		Part-Time Employment	
	Japan	U.S.	Japan	U.S.	Japan	U.S.	Japan	U.S.	Japan	U.S.
Over 3 hrs.	17	3	17	13	2	7	15	33	6	47
2–3 hrs.	19	12	20	20	3	13	9	22	2	10
1–2 hrs.	25	30	33	25	9	28	16	24	2	5
Under 1 hr.	23	38	23	27	55	41	33	15	2	3
No time	15	14	7	12	30	7	27	5	89	32

[1]Percentages are rounded off, and those not responding in various categories are not shown.
Source: Foreign Press Center, *Facts and Figures of Japan* (1980).

the average Japanese adult's allocation of time in daily activities (1975). It includes weekday and Sunday activities for men and women. Table 7 provides some of the data. Students could be asked to draw inferences from these data about work, leisure, and other activities in Japan. Subsequently, they could poll adults in their own communities to generate data to make comparisons. For example, who spends more time watching TV, Japanese or Americans? Men or women?

Activity 2. Secondary   *Facts and Figures* also provides comparative data (page 97 in the 1980 edition) for Japanese and U.S. high school students' daily distribution of time (1977). The composite bar graphs may be difficult for students to read, but teachers could make one or more transparencies of similar graphs to display the information about Japanese students, most of which has been reproduced in Table 8. Students could be asked to interpret the graphs or a table on how the Japanese students spend their time. Then they could be asked to estimate how much time they spend on the same activities. Tally and average students responses on the chalkboard. Ask students:
  · What similarities and differences can you find?
  · What does this suggest about life for Japanese youth as compared to their U.S. counterparts?

Table 9.   Favorite Activities of High School Students

	Japanese Students (%)	U.S. Students (%)
Being With Friends of My Sex	45.1	11.5
Being With Friends of the Opposite Sex	11.8	40.5
Time Spent Alone	16.5	9.8
Time Spent With Family	7.1	11.9
School Club Activities	8.1	5.6
Non-School Club Activities	2.9	6.4

Source: Foreign Press Center, *Facts and Figures of Japan* (1980).

Activity 3. Secondary   Data on favorite activities of Japanese high school students (1978) appear on page 98 of the 1980 edition of *Facts and Figures*. A partial listing is provided in Table 9. Have students identify their favorite activity using the categories in Table 9. Tally student responses on the chalkboard and have students analyze the data. Ask them to consider:
 · How do your responses compare to those of other students in the U.S.? To those of students in Japan?
 · What might be some reasons for the greatest difference in the data provided (being with friends of the same sex and being with friends of the opposite sex)?

Activity 4. Middle Grades/Secondary   Create a slide presentation on "Tradition and Change," using slides from one or more of the series available from the International Society for Educational Information (usually available from Japanese consulates) or by making slides from photographs available in textbooks, the May 1981 issue of *Social Education*, back copies of *Japan* or *Japan Pictorial* (available from consulates), or other sources. Focus on family life, dress, land use, village/city life, traditional arts/modern culture, and other topics. Two screen presentations that show contrasts or changes are especially effective. Have students list, categorize, and discuss the implications of the changes.

SUMMARY

Many fine teacher's guides and resources are available for teaching about Japan at the elementary and secondary levels. Linda Wojtan has identified several of these in her chapter. These deal with every conceivable topic. With the rich resources available, there is little reason why the study of Japan cannot be exciting and informative within the range of maturity and ability of almost every student.

CHAPTER EIGHT

Resources and Materials for Teaching About Japan

LINDA S. WOJTAN

Introduction

Somewhere behind quaint teahouses and shiny Hondas lies the real Japan. Getting beyond these conventional symbols of Japan is a goal of many classroom teachers. While by no means easy, this goal is attainable. Fortunately, there are many free and inexpensive resources located in this country and Japan. Locating these resources, however, is potentially a time-consuming task. This section will identify some of the best resources available.

Although some time will be required in contacting these agencies, it will prove well worth the effort. Soon, supplementary pamphlets and films will enhance your classroom and bulletin board. Learning about another culture can be a multi-sensory experience. Attractive maps, colorful posters, appropriate films, and informative bulletin boards can mean the difference between students' simply learning about Japan versus "experiencing" Japan—indeed, even learning *from* Japan.

IN OUR OWN BACKYARDS

Often, some of the best resources—usually those in our own backyards, so to speak—are overlooked. A good place to begin is your local phone directory. A quick scanning of the listings under "Japan," "Japanese," etc. can be very fruitful. Similarly, the Classified Pages can be a source of potential field trips, speakers, etc., when you consult the restaurant, ethnic/fraternal organizations and other such listings. The location and application of these resources are bounded only by one's imagination and creativity.

Within our own communities, there are many overlooked resource persons. Many of our fellow teachers (often seasoned travelers) are an excellent source of slides, materials, information, and impressions. Why not ask the teacher down the hall to share his presentation with your class? Perhaps a team-taught approach can be devised. Similarly, retired persons, especially former teachers, comprise a talent pool which we usually ignore. Asking these persons to take part in your instructional scheme can lead to a mutually beneficial experience. In some cases, travel agents can be an excellent source of information. Especially culture-sensitive individuals might be invited to give presentations. You might thank them by making their brochures available to your colleagues.

Newspapers and periodicals are an obvious and valuable source of current data on Japan. Although one teacher alone cannot possibly peruse a large number of periodicals, an entire class can. Why not ask that students every Monday bring in a current-events article that they've read and summarized? Monday is an especially good day since students have had a chance to glean material from weekly periodicals and newspapers—the Sunday edition, in particular—and they have also had a chance to visit the local library. Often, this assignment can produce positive family "spin-off" as students discuss their articles on Japan with family members. Therefore, by pooling efforts, an entire class can keep up with the contemporary aspects of Japan. This type of information gathering can even be carried out by elementary school students, once they have learned to recognize the word "Japan" in print. After the students have located their articles on Japan, the teacher can take over and "decipher." An additional dividend accruing from this type of activity is that the class bulletin board will be updated weekly.

Advertisements and cartoons in various periodicals are an especially rich visual resource. They are useful for display and also as the basis of an inquiry lesson into the images and stereotypes of Japan that are portrayed. The Japan Air Lines advertisements—especially those showing Japanese cultural realia—are useful for examining cultural differences. Cartoons and caricatures, readily accessible in a variety of periodicals—notably, the *New Yorker*—provide excellent examples of racial stereotypes in the mass media. For example, the graceful teahouses, bowing figures, and ubiquitous cameras depicted in many cartoons all say something about the way we view the Japanese. Further, the language used in these cartoons usually refers to some aspect of the indigenous culture. References to *haiku* (Japanese poetry) or *hara-kiri* (*seppuku*—ritualistic suicide) can serve as a springboard for the study of those subjects.

CLASSROOM "TRAVEL"

Planning a trip to a faraway place such as Japan can be an exciting educational experience for students. A myriad of community resources can be tapped during the course of this activity. Government agencies can provide the latest rate of exchange between the dollar and the yen; restaurants can provide that all-important "pre-travel" taste. "Travel" preparation includes a study of Japanese customs so that the proverbial "shock" will be lessened. If feasible, a corner of the classroom could be devoted to simulating a *ryokan* (Japanese inn) room and serving a traditional meal on *tatami* (Japanese floormats). Travel agents can aid itinerary planning. "Tourist Japanese" can be taught during a few class sessions on the Japanese language. Local Japanese crafts and products can be studied as students plan their souvenir and gift purchases. Finally, at the end of your imaginary trip-planning experience, the class will have moved a considerable psychic distance in understanding the Japanese without having traversed a physical mile.

FREE RESOURCES

Many free print resources and free-loan films are available from a variety of Japanese agencies in this country. Since it would be impossible to list the address and telephone number of each agency's office, the reader should consult his or her local directory or *Free Resources for Teaching About Japan*.[1]

EMBASSY/CONSULATE GENERAL OF JAPAN RESOURCES

An especially useful resource is the series *Facts About Japan*. This series of handouts (4 to 8 pages in length) covers the following topics: Agriculture, Bunraku, Chanoyu—Tea Ceremony, Children and Festivals, Chronological Outline of Japanese History, Constitution of Japan, Education in Japan, Energy Use in Japan, Gagaku, Geography of Japan, Government, Ikebana, Imperial Family, Industrial Relations, Iron and Steel Industry, Japan's Economy, Kabuki, Literature, Music in Japan, National Flag and Anthem, Noh and Kyogen, Religion, Shipbuilding Industry, Sports in Japan, Status of Women, and Transportation.

---

[1]Linda S. Wojtan, *Free Resources for Teaching About Japan* (Bloomington, IN: East Asian Studies Center, 1979). Available free of charge to classroom teachers.

Other useful publications are: *Facts and Figures of Japan*, an annually updated statistical survey of Japan's geography, population, industry, economy, and national life; and *The Japan of Today*, a comprehensive book covering aspects of modern Japan. Numerous suggestions and resources for introducing Japan into the curriculum are given in *Japan in the American Classroom*. In addition, the following titles are available: *Japan in Transition, Development of Environmental Protection in Japan, Japanese and Americans in a New World in a New Age, Fisheries of Japan*, and *Introducing Japan Through Books: A Selected Bibliography*.

An extensive free-loan film library is maintained by every Japanese consulate office. These 16mm color English language films are available on a free-loan basis, with the user paying only return postage (usually around $4.00). The following list of titles (with running time indicated in parentheses) is offered as a sampling and is by no means exhaustive:

Akiko—the Life of a Japanese Girl (22); Architecture of Japan (20); Art and Meaning of Ikebana (27); Boy and a Crane (27); Bunraku— Puppet Theatre (28); Children's Songs of Japan (29); Family of Tokyo (20); Festival Japan (21); Four Seasons for Children (25); Imperial Family of Japan (27); Invitation to Traditional Music (25); Kabuki: Classic Theatre (32); Kaguya-Hime: The Princess of Moon (18); Language of Japan (20); Modern Women of Japan (27); Origami: Folding Paper (26); Schooling for Progress: Japanese Compulsory System (22); Sports in Japan (23); Children in Town and Village (28); Energy Problem (10); Growing Up Japanese (25); Recreation, Japanese Way (28); Shinkansen Super Express (22); Tokyo: World's Safest City (25).

What I Want To Know About Japan—Brief Answers to Questions Asked About Japan by American Junior High School Students, by Betty Bullard, David T. Lemon, and Timothy Plummer does just what it promises—answers a myriad of questions grouped under more than 25 different topic areas. The engaging narrative of this 80-page booklet is designed to stimulate student interest, while the 8 1/2" × 11" format facilitates duplication for classroom use. A rich array of black-and-white photos enhance and explicate the narrative, and a foldout map is also included. The booklet, commissioned by the Japan Information Center, is an attempt to update many of the changes that have occurred in Japanese society and to provide U.S. teachers with insights and information suitable for an introductory course on contemporary Japan. The topics covered were suggested by 7th grade students from several parts of the United States during an informal survey. The publication is available free of charge from the Japan Information Center, Consulate General of Japan, 153 E. 53rd St., New York, NY 10022.

JAPAN EXTERNAL TRADE ORGANIZATION

A number of print materials and free-loan films are available from the Japan External Trade Organization's regional offices—the Japan Trade Centers. One of the more provocative titles available is *The High Cost of Not Doing Business With Japan.* These free-loan films are distributed nationally through Association Films (formerly known as Association-Sterling).[2] Some of the more useful titles and their order numbers are:

Stories of Four Japanese (F-049); 100 Million Varied Consumers (G-554); Live on Forever—Oze Park (G-553); The Sea and the Japanese (G-552); Decision Making in Japan (K-813); Design—Human Life and Material Things (K-295); Koji, a Young Mechanic (K-815); Where is the Real Japan? (K-297); Meet the Japanese (F-047); On-the-Job Training in Japan (L-911); A Boy and His River (L-910).

JAPAN NATIONAL TOURIST ORGANIZATION

A number of useful pamphlets and films are available from the Japan National Tourist Organization. Some of the most useful pamphlets are *The Tourist's Handbook* and *Your Guide to Japan.* Consult your local directory for phone numbers and addresses of the many branch offices.

PUBLICATIONS: SPECIAL ISSUES ABOUT JAPAN

"Teaching About Japan Through Art and Modern Literature," a Special Section in the May 1981 issue of *Social Education,* contains excellent material for infusing a humanities perspective into the study of Japan. Art is used as a medium for introducing social studies classes to the realities of history. Similarly, literature is introduced so that social studies teachers can break loose from the political-economic-statistical moorings that often delimit courses about contemporary Japan.

The Georgia Social Science Journal, Summer 1981 (Vol. 12, No. 3), features a special issue devoted to Japan. A series of articles present ideas and teaching suggestions which provide some fresh perspectives for those educators who wish to improve the teaching of Japan in the elementary and secondary schools. For example, the importance of studying Japan while incorporating a global perspective is considered.

---

[2]Association Films, Inc. Regional film centers: 600 Grand Avenue, Ridgefield, NJ 07657; 5797 New Peachtree Road, Atlanta, GA 30340; 512 Burlington Avenue, La Grange, IL 60525; 8615 Directors Row, Dallas, TX 75247; 7838 San Fernando Road, Sun Valley, CA 91352

Similarly, the *Southwestern Journal of Social Education*, Fall/ Winter 1980 (Vol. 11, No. 1), adopted the theme "Teaching About Japan." This issue contains a number of teaching lessons about Japan designed to be used directly in the classroom. The lessons focus on concepts and skills useful in all social studies classes.

University-based Outreach Services and Museums

The following outreach programs strive to meet the needs and requests of individuals in pre-collegiate education, business, media, the general community and institutions of higher learning. The conducting of workshops, preparation of materials, and evaluation of existing instructional materials comprise the operations of most outreach programs. While each program does try especially to serve the needs of its particular region of the country, all disseminate information nationwide. The address, telephone number, and contact person for some of the largest centers in this country are contained in the reference section. A number of programs are highlighted below.

In addition, almost all of the outreach programs have free newsletters which they distribute nationwide. These newsletters are often an excellent source of resources, teaching ideas, and information on professional advancement opportunities. Simply write to the outreach coordinator and ask that your name be added to the mailing list.

Stanford University. Among the most useful materials available from Teaching Japan in the Schools (TJS) is *East Meets West: Mutual Images*, a curriculum unit ($30.50). The unit is designed to explore issues of cultural contact. Through examination of the encounters between Japan and the West from the earliest contact (16th Century) to the present, the unit traces various sources of past cultural conflict and misunderstanding. The packaged unit contains 30 slides and a slide script, class set of student handouts, procedural suggestions for classroom activities which include fine supplementary ones, as well as other materials. Although this unit was designed primarily for use at the secondary level, many of the materials have been successfully adapted to the pre-secondary level (grades 6–8).

Also useful is *Seeing the World in a Grain of Sand: The Haiku Moment*, a revised introduction to haiku as a poetry form, focusing on in-class writing activities. The unit is appropriate for creative writing or poetry classes, as well as social studies classes. Accompanying slides and cassette tape set the mood for composing haiku.

Japanese aesthetic principles are also discussed and illustrated by slides from a variety of art forms. Slides only—$1.00; cassette tape only—$3.25; teacher's guide—$3.25; supplementary slide/cassette tape set—$20.50. An elementary version of this resource is also available: teacher's guide—$2.25; slides only—$7.00; cassette tape only—$3.25; supplementary slide/cassette tape set—$12.50.

Castle Towns: An Introduction to Tokugawa, Japan is a slide/text unit developed for high school history, geography, and world culture classes. TJS has designed a unit which allows students to enter the world of the Japanese castle and the society it dominated. They discover why and how castles were built during the Japanese feudal period, and what kinds of people lived in the towns that grew up around them. "Hands-on" activities like the "castle town maze," as well as primary readings and other more analytical assignments, bring the people and values of the era to life. The unit also provides an excellent comparison to Medieval Europe, to which feudal Japan bears striking similarities. The complete kit is $30.50; text only—$5.50; 42-slide set only—$25.00.

University of Illinois. Perhaps one of the most useful activity books available is *Tanoshii Gakushu—Learning with Enjoyment* by Michele Shoresman and Waunita Kinoshita ($8.00). This resource is an excellent compilation of activities and information for grades 1–6, designed to help teachers integrate Japan into various aspects of the existing curriculum. Activities cover such topics as Japanese arts, games, food, folktales, geography and Japan-U.S. trade. All exercises are well explained, adaptable to different levels, and suitable for immediate use. Worksheets may be duplicated for classroom use.

Indiana University. *Free Resources for Teaching about Japan* by Linda S. Wojtan has proved to be a useful resource for teachers. It contains: (1) ideas and suggestions for enriching the study of Japan; (2) information on various organizations and agencies that supply free resources; (3) a listing of print material and film titles currently available; (4) a guide to the use of free Japanese materials in the curriculum and actual classroom strategies and activities.

Indiana is also the home of the Japan-U.S. Textbook Study Project. This binational project has assessed the coverage which each nation accords the other in their respective textbooks. Both junior high and senior high textbooks were examined. Copies of the final report are available from the Social Studies Development Center, 2805 E. 10th Street, Bloomington, IN 47405. Tel. (812) 335-3838.

Beyond the errors and omissions identified and the prescriptive measures recommended looms the question: What immediate application does the Japan-U.S. Textbook Study Project have for classroom teachers? How can the work of scholars involved in the project find its way into the daily classroom routine? Even a quick scanning of the Japan-U.S. Textbook Study Project Report reveals the need for supplementary classroom materials.

The project will be producing a publication that will provide information and examples of activities that would help teachers overcome some of the errors and omissions found in the U.S. treatment of Japan. Contact the Social Studies Development Center for additional information.

Oberlin College. The Outreach Program has prepared the following materials for teaching about Japan at the elementary level: (1) "Visiting Japan—A Second Grade Unit," by Twila Strinka ($3.00); (2) "Art Projects to Enrich a Unit on Japan for Second or Third Graders," by Betty L. Fine ($3.00); (3) "Japan: An Experience Approach to the Study of Japan for Elementary Reading Students," by Susan McConagha ($4.00); (4) "Japanese Garden," by Edith Robinson ($3.00) (includes a small coloring book conveying basic concepts); (5) "Japanese Family Life," by Rose M. Nichols ($2.00) (day-by-day plans for teaching first and second graders about Japan). In addition, the outreach coordinator has prepared an extensive 11-page handout entitled, "Selected Resources for a Unit on Japan in Elementary School." Many of the items listed in the handout are available from Oberlin's free-loan collection.

The Texas Program for Educational Resources on Asia (TEXPERA) at the University of Texas is an especially active outreach program. In addition to an informative free newsletter, the program offers a large library collection of resources (both print and audio-visual available for two-week free-loan period). Included in the collection is the 4-part filmstrip/cassette series *Japan:* (1) *The Present and Past;* (2) *Beliefs, Values;* (3) *Super-business, Daily Life;* (4) *Nature, the Arts, and Leisure.* Also included in the collection is a 2-part, 120-slide collection. Part 1 contains slides of geographic, fishing, historical, and urban scenes. Part 2 consists of selected slides depicting agriculture, industrial, and cultural scenes.

TEXPERA has a number of useful handouts on Japan available free of charge: "Japanese Language and Literature," "Pulling Together a Unit on Japan," "Japan Through Children's Literature," "Reading List for Junior High School Students: A Bibliography for the Study of Japan." It also distributes free of charge: TEXPERA Guide to Asian Studies Resources in Texas; "Addresses of Asian Embassies in the U.S.," "Bibliography of Introductory Texts on Asia," textbook evaluations of *Afro-Asian World: A Cultural Understanding* (Allyn and Bacon) and *Men and Nations: A World History* (Harcourt, Brace and Jovanovich).

University of Washington. The University of Washington Outreach Program has been especially active in providing teacher workshops and continuing education courses for educators in the Northwest. In addition, it has published an audio-visual guide with useful annotations. Elaine Magnusson, an area teacher, was a 1980 recipient of a JISEA fellowship (a coopeative NCSS program). As a result, she has developed an extensive nine-part unit, "Japan—Activities for Elementary School," suitable for grades 4–6. The material is interesting, attractive, and activity-oriented. An exciting aspect of this unit is the artifact exchange box. Through a selection process which promoted values, group work, and cultural identification, Ms. Magnusson's classes assembled an artifact box which she delivered to Japan. In exchange, Ms. Magnusson returned with a wide array of articles suited to children's needs to touch, smell, and explore objects. Information on setting up individual exchange projects is also included.

Another area teacher, Margaret Bigford, has developed an extensive unit entitled "Doing a Japanese Cultural Festival: A 7th Grade World Cultures Unit." The unit is very ambitious, allowing teachers to adapt as they see fit.

Specialized Groups

A number of other organizations in this country and Japan offer useful resources and services. Details are given in the reference section.

International Society for Educational Information. In Japan, the preparation of materials for use in United States schools is spearheaded by the International Society for Educational Information (ISEI). This organization, founded in Tokyo more than 20 years ago, seeks to correct erroneous and outdated information about Japan used in schools around the world. ISEI has produced many materials, including a colorful, interesting and informative elementary school teaching kit. This kit includes: a child's kimono and sash; geta shoes; a Daruma Good Luck doll; two large charts for teaching Chinese characters and Japanese phonetic syllables; calligraphy paper, ink, and brush (for 30 students); origami paper and instructions (for 30 students); wooden chopsticks (for 30 students); a Boy's Day carp fish banner; a furoshiki scarf for wrapping objects; and others. Also included are eight 9″ × 12″ photos showing the above objects in actual use and a teacher's manual explaining the photos and objects in depth, as well as suggesting various interesting classroom, lunchtime, and recess activities using the objects. This kit is available at a below-production price of $50.00. Also available are a four-poster teaching kit, "The Children of Japan," depicting Japanese children at school, at home, at play, and at festivals, and a variety of slide sets.

The Asia Society. The Education Department of the Asia Society strives to promote the study of Asia in the basic pre-collegiate curriculum. It provides support for teachers in planning, content, methodology, and evaluation, and has published a variety of books and film resource guides. One such publication is *Asia in American Textbooks*, a 36-page booklet describing the findings of the Textbook Evaluation Project's two-year study of 306 elementary and secondary social studies books. A related resource is *Highly Rated Elementary and Secondary Social Studies Books* ($1.30). This booklet, prepared by the Textbook Evaluation Project, contains brief descriptions of outstanding books for grades 1–12.

An extremely useful publication of the Asia Society is *Opening Doors: Contemporary Japan* ($6.00). This resource manual contains teaching strategies and readings appropriate for the middle and secondary school. Designed by a team from the United States and Japan, it is organized around the themes of the binational U.S.-Japan Secondary School Project to improve mutual understanding: Utilization of Natural and Human Resources, Decision-Making, Perception and Expression, and Identity and Values. Each thematic unit is geared to stimulating both teacher and student appreciation of Japan and the Japanese. The material draws on aspects of everyday life common to students in the U.S. While the specific material relates to Japan, the theme and the method can be applied to the United States or another country or culture. Since the units are largely self-contained and limited, they do not depend on "coverage" of other materials; however, they can and should be linked to standard curricula and standard texts. The units are intended to help break down barriers between literature and social studies and between humanities and history. These units identify some of the salient themes in contemporary life in the United States and Japan that can help teachers and students to develop a realistic and contemporary image of the Japanese.

The Asia Society is the publisher of *FOCUS on Asian Studies,* a new magazine created to reach out to educators, professionals, and Asia aficionados looking for a comprehensive source journal on Asia. A newly expanded format features articles, essays, book reviews, model curriculum studies and multimedia teaching sources, graphics and photographs for home and classroom use, and a calendar of major cultural events across the country—including museum exhibits, concerts, and performing arts tours. Subscriptions are $5.00 per year for three issues.

The Japanese-American Curriculum Project. This organization has spearheaded the identification of low-cost teaching materials. While its primary function is the development and dissemination of Asian-American curriculum materials, JACP also provides curriculum development assistance, in-service training personnel, and a resource library for teachers and students. The collection of inexpensive materials for the elementary level is large and features many hands-on activities. The collection includes bilingual reading materials, study prints, Asian-American dolls, filmstrips, and even educational comics from Japan. A catalogue is available upon request.

The Japan Society. Especially useful is the pamphlet *What Shall I Read on Japan? The Japanese,* a nationally acclaimed award-winning trilogy of film portraits, is also available for purchase or rental. Part I, *Full Moon Lunch,* captures the everyday life of a downtown Tokyo family who caters elaborate box lunches for memorial services and other formal occasions at nearby Buddhist temples; Part II, *The Blind Swordsman,* depicts Zato-chi, the intrepid blind swordsman, living on the very brink of life yet outrageously confident that he is at life's center. Part III, *Farm Song,* presents four generations of a rural Japanese family who speak frankly about their backbreaking work, their relationships with each other, and the seasonal celebrations that enliven their work. In addition, a variety of other materials are available.

Beyond Textbooks

According to the Japan-U.S. Textbook Study Project, many of our textbooks are guilty of a rather disturbing portrayal of Japan. Typically, we find Commodore Perry, shrouded in a somewhat messianic light, proffering the fruits of Westernization. Another ubiquitous scenario presents the militaristic Japanese running amuck in the 1930s. Various aspects of Japanese culture are similarly maligned, leading one reviewer to exclaim, "Buddhism takes a beating." Such a narrow, skewed presentation of Japan does not serve our students well. Area studies, global studies, and cross-cultural studies are all useful only when they equip our students with skills for life in the 21st Century. Perhaps the most important of these is acceptance of diversity. No matter where our students live, they will daily face many different people with different faiths, customs, and languages. In addition, they will live in an increasingly technological society. Therefore, knowledge of other peoples and places is no longer a luxury, but rather a pragmatic life skill.

A Few Gems. In addition to the numerous resources noted above, a few additional books deserve mention. *Japan As Number One,* by Ezra Vogel,[3] is one of the best resources on the contemporary Japanese phenomenon sometimes referred to as "Japan Inc." Vogel explains that the Japanese, once diligent students of U.S. management practices, are now the teachers. *Japan As Number One* is subtitled "Lessons for America." The book lives up to this claim, as it chronicles in deft prose the history and substance of each "lesson" presented.

No resource listing would be complete without at least a brief mention of Sy Fersh's "classic," *Asia: Teaching About/Learning From.*[4] Fersh believes that Asian studies can and should be more than a subject area—i.e., that students can benefit from the opportunity of learning *from* as well as *about* Asia. With these complementary objectives in mind, he proposes that Asian studies be used in different ways at different levels: (1) elementary grades—emphasis on "the student as the subject," with selected content from Asian studies used to help students develop personal kinds of awareness and appreciation; (2) junior high school—shift to "the process as the subject," where selected Asian studies can help students perceive relationships within a culture and apply these insights to their own behavior; (3) high school—students will be prepared to focus on "the content as the subject" and will be able to learn about and understand in detail any particular culture.

An equally useful resource for teaching about Asia is the 16 mm color/sound film, *Teaching About Japan.* This is not a film about Japan, but rather a demonstration teaching film with the emphasis on teaching about other cultures. The film demonstrates some introductory conceptual sequences that are starting points or "openers" for a study of Japan or any other culture. The ideas presented in the film can be developed into lessons useful at almost any grade level. This film is not intended for passive viewing, since viewers are expected to engage in participatory activities during interrup-

---

[3]Ezra Vogel, *Japan As Number One* (New York: Harper and Row, 1980) $4.95—paperback.
[4]Seymour Fersh, *Asia: Teaching About/Learning From* (New York: Teachers College Press, 1978) $6.95.

tions in the film viewing. In addition, a 27-page viewer's guide accompanies the film. It suggests various teaching strategies and lists numerous organizations. Both the film and teaching guide are available from any of the university-based outreach centers listed in the "References" section.

TRAVEL

There is perhaps no substitute for firsthand study and travel in a foreign culture. Currently, there are a number of programs which offer such opportunities to educators. The National Council for the Social Studies administers teacher travel scholarships to Japan in cooperation with both the Japan Institute for Social and Economic Affairs (JISEA) and the Japan Foundation. Similarly, Youth for Understanding (YFU) has an extensive program of high school student exchanges with Japan. Student exchange scholarships from YFU are available through a special NCSS-administered program.

A FINAL WORD

As mentioned earlier, an acceptance of diversity is perhaps the most important life skill we can foster in our students. The study of Japan offers an opportunity for the examination and study of diversity. A thoughtful study of Japan, stripped of bizarre, exotic, and aberrant images, will not only enrich the lives of our students, but encourage them to abandon ethnocentrism and "learn from" others.

REFERENCES

Amherst College, East Asian Studies Program, Amherst, MA 01002. Carol Angus, Coordinator. Tel.: 413-253-9397.

Asia Society, Inc., Education Department, 725 Park Avenue, New York, NY 10021. Timothy Plummer, Director. Publisher of *Opening Doors: Contemporary Japan.* and *FOCUS on Asia Studies.* Tel.: 212-288-6400

East Asian Curriculum Project, Columbia University, East Asian Institute, 420 W. 118th Street, New York, NY 10027. Roberta Martin, Outreach Coordinator. Tel.: 212-280-4278

Harvard University, Children's Museum, East Asian Education Project, Jamaica Way, Boston, MA 02130. Leslie Swartz, Coordinator. Tel.: 617-426-6500

Indiana University, East Asian Studies Center, 348 Goodbody Hall, Bloomington, IN 47405. Tel.: 812-335-3838

International Society for Educational Information, Kikuei Building, No. 7–8, Shintomi 2-chome, Chuo-ku, Tokyo, Japan 104

JACP, 414 E. Third Avenue, San Mateo, CA 94401. Tel.: 415-343-9408

Japan Society, Inc., Education Department, 333 E. 47th Street, New York, NY 10017. Peter Grilli, Director. Tel.: 212-832-1155

Oberlin College, East Asian Studies, King Building 141, Oberlin, OH 44704. Bobbie Carlson, Coordinator. Tel.: 216-775-8313

Ohio State University, School and Community Outreach Program on Asia, 308 Dulles Hall, 230 West 17th Avenue, Columbus, OH 43210. Leslie Bedford, Coordinator. Tel.: 614-422-9660

Princeton University, East Asian Studies, 211 Jones Hall, Princeton, NJ 80540. Robert Ainspac, Coordinator. Tel.: 609-452-4276

Stanford University, Teaching Japan in the Schools (TJS), Room 200, Lou Henry Hoover Building, Stanford, CA 94305. Kay Sandberg, Coordinator. Tel.: 415-497-1114

University of Arizona, Department of Oriental Studies, East Asia Center, Old Law Building, Tucson, AZ 85721. Ruth Patzman, Coordinator. Tel.: 602-626-5463

University of Hawaii at Manoa, East Asian Language and Area Center, Moore Hall 315, 1890 East-West Road, Honolulu, HI 96822. Valerie Wong, Coordinator. Tel.: 808-948-8543

University of Illinois, Center for Asian Studies, 1208 W. California, Urbana, IL 61801. Jane Gleason, Coordinator. Tel.: 217-333-4850

University of Michigan, Project on East Asian Studies in Education, Center for Japanese Studies, 108 Lane Hall, Ann Arbor, MI 48104. David H. Stark, Coordinator. Tel.: 313-764-5109

University of Texas, Center for Asian Studies, TEXPERA (Texas Program for Educational Resources on Asia), SSB 310, Austin, TX 78712. Louise Flippin, Coordinator. Tel.: 512-471-5811

University of Virginia, East Asian Language and Area Center, Charlottesville, VA 22901. Mary Israel, Coodinator. Tel.: 804-295-1808

University of Washington, East Asian Resource Center, Thomson Hall, DR 05 Seattle, WA 98195. Mary Hammond Bernson, Coordinator. Tel.: 206-543-1921

Yale University, Council on East Asian Studies, Box 13A, Yale Station, New Haven, CT 06520. Constance O'Connell, Coodinator, Tel.: 203-432-4029

Youth for Understanding, 3501 Newark Street, N.W., Washington, DC 20016. Judee Blohm. Tel.: 800-424-3691

Index

Set in 10 pt. Caledonia and printed by Edwards Brothers, Inc. Designed by E. S. Qualls. Indexed by Leila Cabib. Calligraphy by Takeo Ichimuro.